Teen Rights and Freedoms

Social Networking

TEEN RIGHTS AND FREEDOMS

Social
Networking

Roman Espejo
Book Editor

GREENHAVEN PRESS
A part of Gale, Cengage Learning

GALE
CENGAGE Learning·

Detroit • New York • San Francisco • New Haven, Conn • Waterville, Maine • London

Elizabeth Des Chenes, *Managing Editor*

© 2012 Greenhaven Press, a part of Gale, Cengage Learning

Gale and Greenhaven Press are registered trademarks used herein under license.

For more information, contact:
Greenhaven Press
27500 Drake Rd.
Farmington Hills, MI 48331-3535
Or you can visit our Internet site at gale.cengage.com.

ALL RIGHTS RESERVED
No part of this work covered by the copyright herein may be reproduced, transmitted, stored, or used in any form or by any means graphic, electronic, or mechanical, including but not limited to photocopying, recording, scanning, digitizing, taping, Web distribution, information networks, or information storage and retrieval systems, except as permitted under Section 107 or 108 of the 1976 United States Copyright Act, without the prior written permission of the publisher.

For product information and technology assistance, contact us at:

Gale Customer Support, 1-800-877-4253.
For permission to use material from this text or product, submit all requests online at www.cengage.com/permissions.

Further permissions questions can be emailed to permissionrequest@cengage.com.

Articles in Greenhaven Press anthologies are often edited for length to meet page requirements. In addition, original titles of these works are changed to clearly present the main thesis and to explicitly indicate the author's opinion. Every effort is made to ensure the Greenhaven Press accurately reflects the original intent of the authors. Every effort has been made to trace the owners of copyrighted material.

Cover Image © Tom Wang/Shutterstock.com.

LIBRARY OF CONGRESS CATALOGING-IN-PUBLICATION DATA

Social networking : understanding the legal issues of social networking sites / [edited by] Roman Espejo.
    p. cm. -- (Teen rights and freedoms)
    Includes bibliographical references and index.
    ISBN 978-0-7377-5832-0 (hardback)
    1. Online social networks--Law and legislation--United States. 2. Internet--Law and legislation--United States. 3. Cyberbullying--United States--Prevention. 4. Internet and teenagers--United States. 5. Technology and law. I. Espejo, Roman, 1977-
    KF390.5.C6S64 2011
    343.7309'944--dc22
                                                                2011016581

Printed in the United States of America
3 4 5 6 7 15 14 13

Contents

A college student recalls how a cyberbully on Facebook impersonated and harassed her online—nearly sabotaging her college scholarship and career—and how it changed her perceptions of social networking.

Foreword

*"In the truest sense freedom cannot be
bestowed, it must be achieved."*
*Franklin D. Roosevelt,
September 16, 1936*

The notion of children and teens having rights is a relatively recent development. Early in American history, the head of the household—nearly always the father—exercised complete control over the children in the family. Children were legally considered to be the property of their parents. Over time, this view changed, as society began to acknowledge that children have rights independent of their parents, and that the law should protect young people from exploitation. By the early twentieth century, more and more social reformers focused on the welfare of children, and over the ensuing decades advocates worked to protect them from harm in the workplace, to secure public education for all, and to guarantee fair treatment for youths in the criminal justice system. Throughout the twentieth century, rights for children and teens—and restrictions on those rights—were established by Congress and reinforced by the courts. Today's courts are still defining and clarifying the rights and freedoms of young people, sometimes expanding those rights and sometimes limiting them. Some teen rights are outside the scope of public law and remain in the realm of the family, while still others are determined by school policies.

Each volume in the Teen Rights and Freedoms series focuses on a different right or freedom and offers an anthology of key essays and articles on that right or freedom and the responsibilities that come with it. Material within each volume is drawn from a diverse selection of primary and secondary sources—journals, magazines, newspapers, nonfiction books, organization newsletters, position papers, speeches, and government documents, with a particular emphasis on Supreme Court and lower court decisions. Volumes also include first-person narratives from young people and others involved in teen rights issues, such as parents and educators. The material is selected and arranged to highlight all the major social and legal controversies relating to the right or freedom under discussion. Each selection is preceded by an introduction that provides context and background. In many cases, the essays point to the difference between adult and teen rights, and why this difference exists.

Many of the volumes cover rights guaranteed under the Bill of Rights and how these rights are interpreted and protected in regard to children and teens, including freedom of speech, freedom of the press, due process, and religious rights. The scope of the series also encompasses rights or freedoms, whether real or perceived, relating to the school environment, such as electronic devices, dress, Internet policies, and privacy. Some volumes focus on the home environment, including topics such as parental control and sexuality.

Numerous features are included in each volume of Teen Rights and Freedoms:

- An annotated **table of contents** provides a brief summary of each essay in the volume and highlights court decisions and personal narratives.
- An **introduction** specific to the volume topic gives context for the right or freedom and its impact on daily life.
- A brief **chronology** offers important dates associated with the right or freedom, including landmark court cases.
- **Primary sources**—including personal narratives and court decisions—are among the varied selections in the anthology.
- **Illustrations**—including photographs, charts, graphs, tables, statistics, and maps—are closely tied to the text and chosen to help readers understand key points or concepts.

- An annotated list of **organizations to contact** presents sources of additional information on the topic.
- A **for further reading** section offers a bibliography of books, periodical articles, and Internet sources for further research.
- A comprehensive subject **index** provides access to key people, places, events, and subjects cited in the text.

Each volume of Teen Rights and Freedoms delves deeply into the issues most relevant to the lives of teens: their own rights, freedoms, and responsibilities. With the help of this series, students and other readers can explore from many angles the evolution and current expression of rights both historic and contemporary.

Introduction

In June 1997, when the US Supreme Court ruled that the First Amendment applies to online speech, it described the World Wide Web as "a unique medium—known to its users as 'cyberspace'—located in no particular geographical location but available to anyone, anywhere in the world, with access to the Internet."[1] More than a decade later, as high-profile cases involving social networks with sexual victimization, cyberbullying, student expression, and privacy captured the attention of Capitol Hill and the nation, the rights and freedoms of young users remain unsettled and ambiguous.

As child predators surfaced on MySpace and other sites in the mid-2000s, some policy makers attempted to restrict youths' access to social networks at schools and libraries that receive e-funding for Internet services. In May 2006, Representative Mike Fitzpatrick introduced the Deleting Online Predators Act (DOPA) in the House of Representatives. Fitzpatrick argued that such sites are "a feeding ground for child predators" that "lack proper controls to protect their younger users."[2] Although DOPA was passed almost unanimously by the House in July 2006, it stalled in the Senate. The bill was reintroduced by Representative Ted Stevens a year later with the Protecting Children in the 21st Century Act, but it was not voted on by the House or Senate. Since then, public schools and libraries have adopted their own policies and levels of Internet filtering, and social networks set up safeguards against predators and victimization.

Although it did not reach the Supreme Court, *United States v. Drew* is regarded as a pivotal case in cyberbullying laws. In October 2006, Megan Meier, a thirteen-year-old from Dardenne Prairie, Missouri, killed herself after being targeted in an Internet hoax. Angry that Meier had supposedly gossiped about her daughter, Lori Drew contacted the teen on MySpace posing as "Josh," an eighteen-year-old boy, with the help of her daughter and an employee. After a month of flirtation, Josh's exchanges took a cruel twist, including the public posting of private messages. The last message to Meier stated that "The world would be a better place without you."[3] In May 2008, Drew was charged with felony conspiracy and computer fraud by a federal grand jury in California, the location of MySpace's servers. That November, she was found guilty of three misdemeanors; Drew's employee, Ashley Grills, had testified under immunity that she, not Drew, conceived of the hoax and sent the last message. Eight months later, Judge George H. Wu threw out the convictions. "If she is to be found guilty of illegally accessing computers," Wu wrote, "anyone who has ever violated the social networking site's terms of service would be guilty of a misdemeanor."[4]

When teen speech on a social network has been on trial, the lower courts have deferred to Supreme Court decisions involving student expression and the First Amendment. In *Tinker v. Des Moines Independent Community School District* (1969), it upheld the right of three Iowa students to peacefully protest the Vietnam War by wearing black armbands: "School officials do not possess absolute authority over their students. Students in school, as well as out of school, are 'persons' under our Constitution."[5] Still, *Tinker* established that such officials could "prescribe and control conduct in the schools" if it causes material and substantial interference, and subsequent cases defined when student expression could be regulated without infringing the First Amendment. In *Bethel School District v. Fraser* (1986), the Supreme Court ruled that speech containing sexual innuendo could be suppressed at school. In *Morse v. Frederick* (2007), it decided that speech promoting drug abuse could be suppressed at school-affiliated activities. Without a Supreme Court decision regarding free speech on social networks, however, the Third Circuit Court of Appeals issued split opinions in two similar cases of students who parodied their principals with fake MySpace profiles and who challenged the constitutionality of their punishments. On the same day in February 2010 the panel in *Layshock v. Hermitage School District*

(2007) affirmed the student's First Amendment rights, whereas the panel in *Snyder v. Blue Mountain School District* (2008) favored the school's authority in preventing campus disruption.

Privacy and prejudice on social networks came to national prominence the same year. In September 2010, Tyler Clementi, an eighteen-year-old freshman at Rutgers University, jumped off a bridge to his death after learning that his roommate, Dharun Ravi, secretly used a webcam to broadcast online his sexual encounter with another male. Ravi watched the streaming video with dorm mate Molly Wei on her computer and announced it on Twitter. The second time he attempted to spy on Clementi, he tweeted, "Anyone with iChat, I dare you to video chat me between the hours of 9:30 and 12. Yes it's happening again."[6] Ravi and Wei were charged with invasion of privacy and transmission of a sex act on the Internet. "Colleges and universities should articulate a zero-tolerance policy for such invasions of privacy," argued a *Washington Post* editorial.[7] Labeling the suicide a hate crime, Steve Goldman of the gay organization Garden State Equality declared that he was "sickened that anyone in our society, such as the students allegedly responsible for making the surreptitious video, might consider destroying others' lives as a sport."[8] In November 2010, the Tyler Clementi Higher Education Anti-Harassment Act was introduced in the House and Senate. It would require federally supported universities and colleges to change their harassment policies, and its introduction caused further debate. Author and lawyer Wendy Kramer claimed, "This bill is not simply redundant; it's repressive, proposing a subjective definition of harassment that's more restrictive of speech and more likely to be applied arbitrarily than the definition formulated by the Supreme Court some ten years ago."[9] It had been reintroduced in March 2011 at the time of press.

The lower courts continue to navigate the complex legal issues of social networking, with outcomes that seem to conflict and send mixed messages to teens about their online rights. "There are consequences—sometimes severe ones—for those who carelessly use or abuse modern technology," observes Thomas A. Jacobs, a former family and juvenile court judge, who adds, "It won't be long before the US Supreme Court steps in and provides direction in this new era."[10] *Teen Rights and Freedoms: Social Networking* examines the impact that approving a friend request or posting a tweet can have upon the civil liberties of the wired generation.

Notes

1. *Reno v. American Civil Liberties Union*, 521 US 844 (1997).
2. ala.org, May 12, 2006. www.ala.org/ala/alonline/currentnews/newsarchive/2006abc/may2006ab/dopa.cfm.
3. *Washington University Law Review*, 87.2, 2010.
4. *People*, July 4, 2009. www.people.com/people/article/0,,20289459,00.html.
5. *Tinker v. Des Moines Independent Community School District*, 393 US 503 (1969).
6. nj.com, October 1, 2010. www.nj.com/news/index.ssf/2010/09/bias_charge_is _considered_for.html.
7. washingtonpost.com, October 1, 2010. www.washingtonpost.com/wp-dyn/content/article/2010/10/01/AR2010100107163.html.
8. *New York Times*, September 29, 2010. www.nytimes.com/2010/09/30/nyregion/30suicide.html.
9. atlantic.com, December 2, 2010. www.theatlantic.com/national/archive/2010/12 /anti-bullying-laws-and-the-misguided-drive-for-social-equality/67322.
10. *Teen Cyberbullying Investigated: Where Do Your Rights End and Consequences Begin?* Minneapolis, MN: Free Spirit Publishing, 2010.

Chronology

February 24, 1969   The Supreme Court issues its opinion in *Tinker v. Des Moines Independent Community School District*, stating that students do not "shed their constitutional rights to freedom of speech or expression at the schoolhouse gate," but that disruptive speech may be regulated by school officials "to prescribe and control conduct in the schools."

July 7, 1986   The Supreme Court rules in *Bethel School District v. Fraser* that a school's disciplinary action against a student who gave a sexually suggestive assembly speech did not violate his First Amendment rights.

February 8, 1996   President Bill Clinton signs the Communications Decency Act (CDA) into law to regulate pornographic materials on the Internet.

1997   The first website with the features of a social network, SixDegrees.com, launches. It shuts down in 2001.

June 26, 1997   The Supreme Court in *Reno v. American Civil Liberties Union* overturns anti-indecency provisions of the CDA, asserting that free speech is protected on the Internet.

October 28, 1998 President Bill Clinton signs the Digital Millennium Copyright Act (DMCA) into law, intended to protect copyrighted materials from online infringement.

February 12, 2001 In *A&M Records v. Napster*, the Ninth Circuit Court of Appeals issues an injunction against file-sharing service Napster to cease distributing copyrighted music on its network. Napster shuts down the following July.

August 2003 The social networking site MySpace is launched.

February 2004 The social networking site thefacebook .com is launched. The name of the site is later changed to Facebook.

May 9, 2006 Representative Mike Fitzpatrick introduces the Deleting Online Predators Act (DOPA) in the House of Representatives. The legislation seeks to prohibit minors from accessing chat rooms and social networks at federally funded schools and libraries.

July 2006 The social networking and microblogging service Twitter is launched.

October 16, 2006 Thirteen-year-old Megan Meier of Dardenne Prairie, Missouri, hangs herself—and dies the next day—after being bullied in a MySpace hoax perpetrated by Lori Drew, the mother of a former friend, along with her daughter and an employee.

January 4, 2007   Representative Ted Stevens reintroduces DOPA in the Senate as part of the Protecting Children in the 21st Century Act, which aims to prevent the distribution of child pornography and sale of minors' personal information in interstate commerce.

June 25, 2007   The Supreme Court rules in *Morse v. Frederick* that student speech promoting drug abuse on campus or at school events is not protected by the First Amendment.

July 10, 2007   In *Layshock v. Hermitage School District*, a federal judge rules that the punishment of a student for parodying his school principal in a MySpace profile violates the First Amendment.

July 24, 2007   The media reports that MySpace has removed more than 29,000 profiles of registered sex offenders from its site.

August 9, 2007   MySpace reaches 100 million profiles worldwide.

September 11, 2008   In *Snyder v. Blue Mountain School District*, a US District Court upholds that the suspension of a student for parodying her school principal in a fake

MySpace profile does not violate the First Amendment.

November 28, 2008   In *United States v. Drew*, a US District Court jury finds Drew not guilty of felony computer-hacking charges and convicts her of three misdemeanors.

July 2, 2009   A federal judge overturns the three convictions against Drew for computer fraud.

February 4, 2010   On appeal in *Layshock v. Hermitage School District*, a Third Circuit panel affirms the ruling that the punishment over MySpace was not within school authority. On the same day, another Third Circuit panel on appeal in *Snyder v. Blue Mountain School District* upholds that disciplinary action was within school authority.

July 21, 2010   Facebook reaches 500 million users worldwide.

September 22, 2010   Rutgers University freshman Tyler Clementi commits suicide after a video of him having sex with another man was secretly streamed online and announced on Twitter by his roommate, Dharun Ravi. Ravi and a dormmate, Molly Wei, are charged with invasion of privacy.

November 18, 2010   Representative Rush Holt and Senator

Frank Lautenberg introduce the Tyler Clementi Higher Education Anti-Harassment Act to Congress. Holt and Lautenberg reintroduce the bill on March 11 the next year.

January 1, 2011   Twitter reaches 200 million registered accounts worldwide with 110 million tweets a day.

*"The law in [social networking] is still
relatively unsettled, but . . . legislation
in motion promises to keep things
interesting for the foreseeable future."*

Understanding the Legal Issues of Social Networking Sites

Kevin Fayle

Kevin Fayle is senior editor at FindLaw, a legal website. In the following viewpoint, Fayle surveys the developing legal obligations and liabilities of social networks and their users. He explains that social networks, under federal laws, are not liable if users post content that violates copyright or is defamatory, but court decisions suggest that social networks can control content in some ways. Users do not enjoy these protections, Fayle continues, and, in key cases, different courts have ruled in favor of or against the First Amendment rights of students who created fake online profiles. In addition to federal laws, the author maintains that several states have enacted or proposed age-verification requirements for minors on social networks.

Kevin Fayle, "Understanding the Legal Issues for Social Networking Sites and Their Users," FindLaw, September 18, 2007. Copyright © 2007 by FindLaw, A Thomson Reuters Business. All rights reserved. Reproduced by permission.

It seems that everyone is a member of a social network these days. Whether it's your kids on MySpace and Facebook, or your colleagues on LinkedIn, people are taking advantage of these new online meeting spaces to make friends, communicate and expand business opportunities.

But what are the legal obligations that arise out of the use of social networks, both for the user and the sites themselves? The law in this area is still relatively unsettled, but some recent [2007] developments have created intriguing precedent, and legislation in motion promises to keep things interesting for the foreseeable future.

Laws Pertaining to Social Networking Sites

The two most important statutes to consider when discussing the legal liabilities and obligations of the social networking sites are Section 512(c) of the Digital Millennium Copyright Act and Section 230 of the Communications Decency Act.

Section 512 Section 512(c) removes liability for copyright infringement from websites that allow users to post content, as long as the site has a mechanism in place whereby the copyright owner can request the removal of infringing content. The site must also not receive a financial benefit directly attributable to the infringing activity.

This creates an interesting problem for most sites that allow users to post music, photos or video. For instance, several content owners have sued YouTube, the video sharing site, for copyright infringement, and YouTube has claimed a 512(c) defense. Since YouTube is a subsidiary of Google, its future business plan most likely involves serving advertisements according to the kind of video that users view or search for. If the site does this, however, it could amount to a financial benefit directly attributable to the sharing of copyrighted materials.

Those cases are currently before federal district courts, and their resolution will greatly impact the services that social networks offer, as well as their business models.

Section 230 Section 230 of the Communications Decency Act immunizes websites from any liability resulting from the publication of information provided by another. This usually arises in the context of defamation, but several courts have expanded it to cover other sorts of claims as well.

Thus, if a user posts defamatory or otherwise illegal content, Section 230 shields the social network provider from any liability arising out of the publication. Websites that, in whole or in part, create or develop contested information, on the other hand, are deemed "content providers" that do not benefit from the protections of Section 230.

A recent 9th Circuit opinion has called the section's broad coverage into question, and created uncertainty for social networking sites that have relied on Section 230 to protect them from claims relating to the content that their users create.

That case, *Fair Housing Council of San Fernando Valley v. Roommates.com, LLC*, began when two fair housing groups sued the website Roommates.com, alleging that Roommates.com's roommate networking service violated the Fair Housing Act. The district court found that the website qualified for Section 230 immunity and entered judgment for the website without reaching the question of whether the site did indeed violate the FHA. On appeal, the Ninth Circuit reversed and remanded for a trial on the merits.

A divided Ninth Circuit panel found that the website created or developed information on the site in two ways: First, by creating the questions that users answered when creating their profiles. Second, by channeling or filtering the profiles according to the answers to those questions.

The court's second justification is fairly controversial, and goes against the widely established precedent granting a broad, robust privilege to interactive service providers. In essence, the panel's ruling holds that, by channeling information to users and providing search capabilities, Roommates.com has added an additional layer of information, "meta-information" you could say, that it is at least partly responsible for creating or developing.

The effects of this new "channeling" test could be devastating for social networking sites, many of which operate in similar ways to Roommates.com. Sites could now find themselves open to liability for information posted by third parties, and this could result in a reduction of the number of speech-related services available online—exactly the opposite of what Congress intended when [approving into law] Section 230 in the first place.

For example, MySpace.com attempts to restrict the ability to view underage profiles by preventing older users from accessing them. In effect, the website filters the content based on answers provided during registration to ensure that only minors of certain ages can view other profiles from that age group. This would almost certainly qualify as meta-information under the Roommates.com decision, and would bump MySpace out from under the protection of Section 230.

If a sexual predator give a false age on MySpace.com and then lured a victim from the site, would MySpace then be open to claims of negligence in the publication of the information? A federal district court in Texas recently answered that question in the negative, but under this new decision, which carries more jurisprudential weight, courts could swing in the opposite direction and find the website liable.

Given that the Roommates.com decision goes against the body of established precedent for Section 230 cases, however, it is likely that Roommates.com will ask for an en banc review, and it is quite possible that they will prevail during that review. Until then, however, watch for a possible deluge of plaintiffs rushing to court in the Ninth Circuit's jurisdictions in order to sue social networking sites.

Social Networking Terms of Use

Most social networking sites address the use of third-party content in their terms of use. For example, Twitter's "Basic Terms" include the statement that users are "solely responsible for . . . any data, text, information, screen names, graphics, photos, profiles, audit and video clips, links" that the user submits, posts or displays. Another Basic Term states that users "must not, in the use of Twitter, violate any laws in your jurisdiction (including but not limited to copyright laws)." Thus, in addition to violating copyright laws, the unauthorized use of third-party content violates the terms of use of most social networking sites and could serve as an additional basis for liability.

Kathryn L. Ossian, "Legal Issues of Social Networking," millercanfield.com.

State Laws In addition to these federal statutes, several states have enacted or proposed laws that would create requirements for social networking sites, particularly in regard to monitoring the presence and activities of sexual predators using the sites.

Virginia, for example, has enacted a law requiring sexual offenders to register their email addresses and IM screen names, and allows police officers to create mechanisms for websites to check user information against the resulting database.

The North Carolina state senate recently passed a bill requiring that parents and guardians register with a social networking site and verify their ages before their children can sign up for an account. This is to counter the difficulty in verifying the ages of minors, who usually lack credit cards or other sources of information concerning their ages. That bill still requires approval from the North Carolina House of Representatives.

Connecticut legislators have also proposed a bill that would require social networking sites to verify the ages of their users and obtain parental permission for users under 18. Under the proposed law, sites that failed to comply would be subject to fines of $5,000 per day.

Legal Considerations for Social Networking Users

Social networking users don't enjoy any of the immunities granted to social networking sites under the law, so they should be careful to always act appropriately when posting messages or files to the sites.

The main areas where users can get themselves into trouble are through the posting of defamatory content or content that infringes on intellectual property rights.

Since no statutory immunities exist to shield users, the standard laws pertaining to defamation and infringement apply.

Users of social networking sites such as Facebook must be careful not to violate any laws. Users frequently experience trouble in the areas of defamatory material and intellectual property infringement. © Thomas Coex/AFP/Getty Images.

If a user is found to have posted defamatory content, the user will be liable, even if the site can escape liability under Section 230. Similarly, if a user posts material that infringes on another's copyright, the user will face liability for the infringement, despite the site's potential safe harbor under Section 512(c).

The First Amendment and state constitutional free-speech provisions often come into play in these types of defamation suits. Several of the most prominent cases regarding user liability for material posted on social networking sites have dealt with students suffering criminal charges or adverse consequences at their schools as a result of allegedly defamatory, threatening or indecent messages posted on social networking sites.

The most important of these recent student cases is a case recently decided by the Indiana Court of Appeals, *A.B. v. State.* In that case, A.B., a minor, posted expletive-filled comments on a fake MySpace page purporting to belong to A.B.'s former middle school principal. The principal reported the site to the authorities, and A.B. was declared a "juvenile delinquent" by a juvenile court after the judge found that the comments constituted criminal harassment.

The Court of Appeals reversed, finding that the free-speech component of the Indiana State Constitution protected the comments that A.B. posted. Since A.B. had challenged the school's anti-piercing policy in her post, the court held, the comment was political speech aimed at the principal's policies, and protected under the Indiana Constitution.

In two other cases, *Layshock v. Hermitage School District* and *[Synder] v. Blue Mountain School District*, the students were not so lucky. In both cases, the school's punishments against students for creating fake MySpace pages in the names of their respective principals were upheld by federal district courts. After the Supreme Court's decision in *Morse v. Frederick*—the infamous "Bong Hits 4 Jesus" case—the decisions are unlikely to be overturned on appeal.[1]

Also keep in mind that many states are passing laws that create obligations to verify a user's age. Any fraud or circumvention of these requirements could have repercussions for social networking users in addition to the usual charges of defamation and infringement.

Note

1. Joseph Frederick unfurled a sign with this slogan outside of his school in 2002. The sign was taken away, and Frederick was suspended. He sued, and his case was eventually heard by the Supreme Court who ruled in favor of the school.

| "There can be no doubt that a child's innocence and perhaps even more can be lost in an instant on the Internet."

Social Networks Should Be Banned at Libraries and Schools

David W. Zellis

In the following viewpoint, David W. Zellis supports the Deleting Online Predators Act (a 2006 bill that failed to become a law) to restrict children's use of social networks at schools and libraries receiving federal funds. Zellis contends that such websites as MySpace and Facebook expose children to online predators, cyberbullying, and street crime—frequently without the knowledge of parents or guardians. Several disturbing cases in Bucks County, Pennsylvania, illustrate the dangers of social networking, the author maintains. Zellis is the first assistant district attorney and chief of community outreach at the district attorney's office in Bucks County.

Thank you for the opportunity to be here today [July 11, 2006] to talk about a serious issue that affects our most treasured resource, our children, and our effort to protect them from

David W. Zellis, "Testimony of Bucks County (PA) First Assistant District Attorney David W. Zellis Before the United States House of Representatives, the Committee on Energy and Commerce, Subcommittee on Telecommunications and the Internet," July 11, 2006.

the dangers of "social networking sites" that exist on the World Wide Web.

As the highest ranking prosecutor next to the elected district attorney, I have spent the past twenty-two (22) years fighting in the courtroom to put criminals behind bars. My courtroom experience involves every type of case, including capital murder. I also work hand in hand with law enforcement [personnel] as they investigate criminal activity. One could say that, during my tenure as a county prosecutor, "I have seen it all." Despite my exposure to all kinds of criminal behavior, I, like many of my colleagues, have been shocked and dismayed by the latest rage, politely known as "social networking sites," but commonly known as MySpace, Friendster, Facebook and Xanga.

Cyberspace Instead of the Street Corner

It was not that many years ago that police arrested, and I prosecuted, child molesters for making advances toward children on the street corner or in the park. It was not that long ago that drug dealing took place on the street corners, and I locked those dealers up, and it was only a short time ago that "bullying" meant beating up a kid on the playground. Times have changed. The internet and these social networking sites have redefined, reinvented and reinvigorated child predators, drug dealers and bullies. Now sexual predators troll the social networking sites rather than the streets and get all the information they need in order to groom children for the ultimate purpose of victimizing them. Drug dealers in suburban communities like Bucks County can now conduct business in cyberspace instead of the street corner. And bullies do not have to throw a punch when they can go on the internet and engage in cyber bullying and inflict more pain and suffering on kids than a fight in the school yard used to cause.

Bucks County, Pennsylvania, is a diverse northern suburb of Philadelphia. With over 600,000 residents, in many ways it represents a typical suburban community. We have areas where

Bullying is common both offline and online, often with equally dangerous results in both cases.
© SW Productions/Photodisc/Getty Images.

crime is higher than other areas, but on the whole the streets of Bucks County are very safe. The information superhighway, however, possesses a significant challenge to law enforcement, schools, parents and legislators, as we try to balance the benefits and the dangers that lurk in cyberspace.

There are four recent cases that occurred in Bucks County that poignantly illustrate the dangers posed by such sites as MySpace. In the first case, a fourteen-year-old boy had his profile posted on MySpace. In April of 2006 he was contacted by a male posing as a teenager, who convinced the fourteen-year-old to lie to this mother and have her drop him off at the local mall. The male met the fourteen-year-old at the mall and then took him to a motel, where he had sexual intercourse with the child. This scenario happened on a number of occasions, and was only discovered when a school official overheard the fourteen-year-old's conversation with a friend and reported it to law enforcement. Following the arrest, the male perpetrator was identified as a twenty-five-year-old. The fourteen-year-old had never been in trouble before, and prior to this had had no sexual experience. The sexual predator now sits in the Bucks County Prison awaiting trial.

The next case is one of the first cases in which law enforcement arrested someone for selling drugs on MySpace. Not only was this juvenile selling drugs on MySpace, but he was pictured on MySpace with an assortment of guns.

The third case involves a thirteen-year-old girl who posted her pictures on MySpace. A male began conversing with her on the internet. Fortunately, the child's mother contacted law enforcement, and the police took over the conversations with this sexual predator and ultimately arrested him. He was identified as a male who was working in an OB/GYN office.

Finally, we have seen street gangs taking advantage of the opportunities provided through social networking sites, and such street gangs as the Bloods and Crips use the sites as a recruitment tool in the suburbs.

No Boundaries

Too often as a society we think that sexual predators and internet crime is somebody else's problem, not ours. Those of us in law enforcement know that nothing could be further from the truth. These four examples, which occurred in Bucks County within the last six months, indicate that the kind of criminal activity in cyberspace knows no boundaries and now happens on a national and international level.

My office is not only prosecuting such cases in court, but we are proactively engaged in prevention activities. We have gone into elementary, middle and high schools to educate students about the dangers involved in social networking sites. We have held town meetings around the county to educate parents about how to keep their children safe on the internet. These programs have been well received by students and parents, and it has become clear to us that parents and most kids do not want pornography or sexual propositions to interfere with their use of the internet

During the course of our town meetings with parents, we have found a hunger on the part of the parents to learn as much as they possibly can, because parents legitimately feel that they are playing "catch up" to their children when it comes to the internet. One of the critical components of the Deleting Online Predators Act is requiring the Federal Trade Commission to create a website which can be used as a resource for parents, teachers and others regarding the dangers on the internet to child users. In addition, the requirement that the Federal Trade Commission issue consumer alerts to parents and others regarding the potential dangers of internet child predators is critical to providing parents and teachers with worthwhile information that they crave. This begins to address one of the most significant concerns, and that is that no one is controlling the information highway.

Finally, with respect to the Deleting Online Predators Act,

ponytail14: i'm registered on myspace.com. r u registered?

boytoy14: yes...i'm registered.

Copyright © 2006 Mike Lester, The Rome News-Tribune and PoliticalCartoons.com.

if you knew that a child molester was going to the library or to a school and grooming children for future sexual exploitation, would you allow such behavior to go on? Of course not. But that is exactly what is going on when children in school or at the library are permitted to freely access commercial networking sites like MySpace and chat rooms, while sexual predators lurk in their midst in cyberspace.

Children's Safety Comes First

We cannot and should not permit our children to fall prey to [exploitation by] sexual predators while they are at school or at the library. We have seen firsthand that when a law enforcement officer poses as a teenager on line, sexually explicit instant messaging and solicitations occur quickly and rampantly. There can be no doubt that a child's innocence and perhaps even more can be lost in an instant on the internet.

On behalf of Bucks County District Attorney Diane E. Gibbons, we wholeheartedly endorse the Deleting Online Predators Act because it educates parents and children about the dangers of the internet and limits access to certain sites during the school day. Our children's safety must come first.

"The arguments for allowing access to social networking sites tend towards information literacy . . . and use of these tools in education."

Social Networks Should Not Be Banned at Libraries and Schools

Lauren Pressley

In the following viewpoint, Lauren Pressley opposes a ban on social networks at public schools and libraries. She argues that the failed Deleting Online Predators Act of 2006 would infringe free speech, disproportionately affect disadvantaged youths, and discourage Internet literacy. Practical issues, Pressley states, from acquiring better filtering software to training staff to enforce policies, must be considered. She instead favors incremental or tiered levels of access to social networks that promote student education and responsibility. The author is the instructional design librarian at Wake Forest University and a member of the North Carolina Library Association Intellectual Freedom Committee.

This paper explores a case study examining the process of making recommendations to a public library director about

Lauren Pressley, "Policy Analysis and Recommendations," Lauren's Library Blog, March 25, 2007. http://laurenpressley.com/library/. Copyright © 2007 by Lauren Pressley. All rights reserved. Reproduced by permission.

what actions they should take regarding teenagers accessing social networking sites from the eight terminals at the library. As such, it is useful to keep in mind the policy cycle which consists of defining the problem, setting the agenda, formulating policy, implementation, and then, possibly restatement of policy or policy termination. In this paper I use this policy cycle to define the problem, set the agenda, and formulate policy.

The American Library Association [ALA] calls the sites under consideration "Interactive Web Applications," which includes interactive web sites and pages that include user-generated content. These sites allow people to share information, [to] collaborate, and to organize. These sites sometimes are utilized in the educational process as well. They provide a way for teachers and librarians to provide feedback, and also give teenagers a way to gain this experience in a safe environment. This safe environment helps prepare students for entering a workforce that is utilizing these technologies for business purposes.

The director is concerned that more teenagers are using the computers to access social networking sites and worries that there are possible safety and liability issues associated with this behavior. These are the parameters of the problem, and I would go on to define the problem as a lack of a way to prevent liability when teenagers are using library computers to access social networking sites. The library may be able to prevent liability with filtering, a better policy, education, or a way to enforce policy. This [viewpoint] will explore these options in the context of stakeholders, legal issues, American Library Association stances, and existing local library policies

Any member of the community with a "vested interest in the library" is a stakeholder. In this specific scenario, the stakeholders are the librarians who have noticed an increase in teenage social networking site use, the teenage patrons using the sites, and the director who brought up this as a situation. Other stakeholders include the teenagers' parents; the other library patrons who are using the computers and might have to wait for computers while the teenagers use the sites; and, indirectly, the public schools, as students might turn to using these computers if they are restricted at the library.

Gathering Necessary Information Is Essential

Before suggesting solutions, there are several pieces of missing information. One is the existing library policy that is posted at each terminal. What are their current rules that the library requires patrons to follow? It is also important to consider the state that the library is located in, as some states are passing strict laws regarding social networking sites. Another factor is the system that the library belongs in, in case there are systemwide policies in place. When thinking about legal implications, it is important to know if the library is receiving e-rate benefits. Finally, it would be worth finding out if there is a legal department for the library, and if so, what their suggestions are regarding liability.

It is also worth examining legal implications. When considering the constitutional issues, it is worth considering the First Amendment of the Bill of Rights. This is the amendment that says that the Congress cannot create legislation that abridges free speech. Since much of participating in social networking sites is about adding content, it could be interpreted as limiting free speech if these sites are [restricted].

After starting from this broad approach, it is useful to look at federal legal issues. The first to consider is the Children's Internet Protection Act, or CIPA. CIPA required any library or school receiving e-rate benefits to use filters to protect users under the age of seventeen from viewing sites that include pornography, obscenity, or are "harmful to minors." Social networking sites are not inherently pornographic, obscene, or harmful to minors, but may contain some content that falls into these categories. When considering CIPA, it is worth examining filters to make sure that they are catching these individual pages on social networking sites that contain the restricted content.

The American Library Association has strenuously objected to the use of filtering software to block websites available to young people in public schools. The organization prefers an approach based on teaching coping skills instead. © AP Images/Carolyn Kaster.

The Deleting Online Predators Act

The Deleting Online Predators Act [DOPA] of 2006 passed the House by a landslide. It passed during a previous session of Congress before reaching the Senate, so was reintroduced in 2007 in the House. This act builds on the Communications Act of 1934 to require all public schools and libraries to "prohibit access to social networking websites on all computers made available to the public." DOPA does not limit [its definition of] social networking sites to MySpace, Facebook, and other social websites in the news. The broad definition of social networking includes any site that allows users to create profiles and accounts such as Amazon and Yahoo or the use of online email, wikis, blogs, and even online courses. DOPA should not necessarily impact library policy at this point in time, since it has not been signed into law yet, but the director should remain aware that new laws might impact the policies that the library must operate under.

The American Library Association has taken a stand in this discussion of policy, based largely on their code of ethics, library bill of rights, and focus on intellectual freedom. The strong stance of this organization was illustrated in a letter to the Senate in opposition to the Deleting Online Predators Act. Members of ALA have also given testimony to the Congress about social networking software in libraries. The executive director of ALA's Young Adult Library Services Association made three main points when testifying, focusing on the ambiguous definition used in DOPA, that DOPA might widen the digital divide, and that education is the best way to help keep kids safe online. ALA has asked members to communicate concerns about DOPA with their senators in hopes that this will help keep DOPA from happening. Finally, the ALA Council has passed a resolution in support of online social networks as well, tying the availability of these sites to the library's role as a place to learn information literacy skills.

There are local perspectives as well. Illinois, Georgia, and North Carolina legislatures are discussing bills that might restrict teenage access to social networking sites. North Carolina, specifically, is considering S.B. 132, the Protect Children From Sexual Predators Act, which has a section that requires "parental permission for minors to access social networking Web sites." Again, as the Protect Children From Sexual Predators Act is not law yet, it should not necessarily inform policy. The director should, however, remain aware of the possibility of this becoming law the potential necessity to incorporate it into library policy.

Practical Issues Must Be Considered

Having this understanding of federal, local, and professional policies, there are also practical issues to consider when examining this situation. On the extremely practical end, it is useful to think about what changes might happen in the workplace if a strict policy was put into place. This could include having to find better filtering software, having to get the staff to behave as enforcing officers, and educating both staff and users about new policies.

There are practical issues to consider when considering potential policy. One consistent argument for keeping access to social networking sites is education. It is probably most effective to teach children how to interact with strangers in real and online worlds, rather than try to keep kids from them altogether. These sites have great potential for education as well. Blogging, social networking sites, course management systems (like Blackboard), and online communication allows for new ways to teach and educate, and restricting those sites keeps these educational options off the table. Finally, blocking these sites in educational institutions means that educators cannot teach students how to interact safely and tell an adult about a problem on social networking sites.

Competitiveness is another practical concern. As businesses begin using social web applications for business purposes, it makes sense to help the future work force understand how to use these sites. A lot of kids are able to access these sites from their homes, but some cannot. This leads us to another practical concern: the digital divide. Economically disadvantaged kids . . . have access to internet [only at school] and at the library, so limiting these sites in these areas means these children will not have exposure to social networking sites.

Finally, it can be useful to look at how local communities are dealing with social networking sites. In North Carolina, there are a broad number of approaches. Wake County has, perhaps, the strictest policies. Beginning March 1, 2007, the public libraries have used [the] filter, "Websense," to block MySpace from their computers. Wake County Libraries are planning to monitor the usefulness of the filter over the next three to six months before deciding if they should take additional actions. Greensboro public libraries take a tiered approach. They suggest that the first defense is for parents to talk with their children, and to use

Social Networking Bans Are Not Enforceable

A ban on a single popular site, like MySpace, would not be enforceable. Clever Digital Natives who wanted to take part in online social networking could easily switch to another online service. It is in fact likely that a brand new service would have fewer protections for kids' safety than MySpace and Facebook, not more. Services like MySpace that have been around for a while are at least working with regulators and advocates for children to improve the safety of their space.

John Palfrey and Urs Gasser, Born Digital: Understanding the First Generation of Digital Natives. *New York: Basic Books, 2008.*

the Internet Safety Pledges as guidelines for internet use. These pledges are different for different age groups. The ages are broken down from kindergarten to second grade, third through sixth grade, and middle and high school. The younger children have more specific and restrictive regulations, while the teenagers' focus more on communicating with elders and understanding expectations. Forsyth County Public Libraries automatically gives the highest level of filtering for all users under the age of seventeen, but offers the option of less filtering if a parent signs a Filtering Options Form. Forsyth County also makes clear that their filters are not one-hundred-percent accurate, and "should not be relied on for complete protection."

There Are Several Options for Libraries

Based on these [examples], we see several options that the library can consider using. Like Wake County, the library could choose to block specific sites, adding additional blocks as necessary. This has the advantage of being incremental. The library can operate slowly, adding sites as necessary and removing sites as unnecessary. However, MySpace has many useful functions including teen book clubs and library sites, so in blocking the site altogether, these [functions] are limited as well.

Like Forsyth, the [library] could offer strong filtering for any teenager, but with an exception if a teenager's parent chooses to change the filtering level. Varying levels of filter could be addressed by using smart cards and parental consent forms. This allows the library to be as strict as it needs to be, but also allows individuals to have personalized levels of filtering as necessary. The main drawback to this is that if some parent is unable to come in due to work, family obligations, or scheduling, they will not be able to change the level of filtering on their child's account.

Like Greensboro, the library could offer a tiered approach, based on some form of a safety pledge. This allows for education and increased levels of responsibility, but also relies on honesty and following rules. This, practically, might require more work on the part of the librarians, too, in terms of changing filtering levels or watching what people are doing on the computers.

Assuming that this library receives federal e-rate funding, the library has to be offering some level of filtering. In addition to this, the library could choose to try to increase parental involvement or offer education for teenagers who want to use these sites. I would recommend some combination of the Greensboro Library policies and an education initiative. I come to this recommendation as a member of the Intellectual Freedom Committee of NCLA. This committee stands behind the ALA values of open access to information and believes that internet filtering is not that different from the censorship of books. The emphasis on education is an important one, as the arguments for allowing access to social networking sites tend towards information literacy, competitiveness in the business market, and use of these tools in education. As such, it will be important to include training and marketing to help teenagers make good choices as they are given more responsibility.

| "Students should not let anyone control their MySpace, but they should be aware of the risks and create their profiles in a responsible, thoughtful way."

Students' Rights on MySpace Should Be Protected

Personal Narrative

Selina Maclaren

In the following viewpoint, Selina Maclaren claims that she is too occupied to use MySpace and has no desire to share personal information on the Internet with strangers. Amid warnings to her classmates to remove profane and provocative content from their MySpace profiles by school faculty and staff, however, Maclaren defends teens' freedom of expression on social networks. Although she does not condone such online conduct, the author argues that schools do not have the right to discipline students or threaten their academic records because of their MySpace profiles. At the time of publication Maclaren was a high school student at West Valley Christian School in West Hills, California.

Last spring [in 2005], when my Bible class teacher spent an entire Sunday looking at every student's MySpace that he could

Selina Maclaren, "Who's Reading Your MySpace?" LA Youth, January–February 2006. Copyright © 2006 by Youth News Service/L.A. Youth. All rights reserved. Reproduced by permission.

find, there was an uproar the following Monday. "Oh that's so gross, he's so nosy. He shouldn't have a right to do that," girls said. Since my school has fewer than 200 high school students, by third period, everyone knew. If anyone was called to the office for innocent reasons, rumors spread that they were going to be suspended because of their MySpace.

During his Bible classes, Mr. Shaw told his students that he had viewed their MySpaces and had seen provocative pictures and vulgar language, and, as students at a Christian school, they should ask themselves if that was the right thing to do. He didn't scold anyone in particular, but everyone wondered, "Was he talking about me?"

While everyone else panicked, I was relieved that I wouldn't have to worry that I had posted something three months ago that I deeply regretted. I don't have a MySpace and I never will.

At first, my not having a MySpace was no big statement. It just wasn't convenient. I was already texting, instant messaging, talking on the phone and trying to keep up with homework in the midst of all this communication. Besides, my Internet access was slow and always crashed when I tried to view MySpace.com, where friends were posting pictures of themselves, their interests and entries about what they've been up to. Then it seemed like one day I woke up and everyone had a MySpace, and I had to become an extremist to hold my ground. People would ask me, "Why don't you have a MySpace?" as if I was a freak of nature. I tried to explain that I thought it was too addicting, too tempting to exploit yourself, a huge cause of unneeded drama, and a total waste of time if you were just talking to the people you saw every day. Besides, how could you possibly have so many "friends" to brag about when you spent all your time sitting in front of your computer? Naturally, I came off sounding like a psycho fanatic. My rants about the ridiculousness of displaying personal emotions to be read by strangers all over the world caused some strange looks and awkward silences.

My school sent home a letter explaining what MySpace

was—a site for networking and communication—and warning parents that students were misusing the site as a place to post suggestive pictures and obscene language. The school encouraged parents to view their children's MySpaces and be aware of the dangers of publicly displayed personal information. After that, it was us against them. I was a MySpace hater, along with the administration and about three other students, and we were supposedly against the whole school. During homeroom, a friend told me that just because she had a MySpace didn't mean she was satanic. I was in a grumpy mood and made the mistake of saying something along the lines of, "MySpace isn't the devil, it's just where demons go to fester in their own bacteria." Later that day, as I walked into Bible class, I saw my words on Mr. Shaw's blackboard for every class to see. Although a lot of people laughed good-naturedly at what I had said and I knew that Mr. Shaw had only displayed it for humor's sake, now everyone in my claustrophobically tiny school would pair me with Mr. Shaw. We were the demon hunters out to evict people from their MySpace homes.

Myspace.com Is Not Bad in Itself

No one understood that I'm not against other people having MySpaces—most of my best friends have them, and I've delicately crept over to their pages a few times, worried that I'll be accused of being a hypocrite, but curious nonetheless. And I agree with them that MySpace in itself is not morally wrong or even very dangerous. MySpace is a tool of communication, and for a lot of people, it is the only way to keep in touch.

So even though I felt that Mr. Shaw had not violated his rights as a teacher, I was uncomfortable that he had made it a personal duty of his to find signs of immorality in something unrelated to the school. In my opinion, parents should teach us morals while schools ought to be a place of opportunity, not restraint. In history class, we are taught to value the famous "life, liberty, and the pursuit of happiness" from America's Declaration of Independence. We are taught how important it is that the First Amendment protects our right to free speech. So when we step into our Bible class, do those rights go away? Of course the right of a teacher to view MySpaces—a publicly displayed domain—cannot be denied. But when does a school's concern become an invasion of students' privacy? Many private schools are dealing with this issue—how can they teach the values of American freedom alongside religious morals, and which will overrule the other? In search of answers, I interviewed Mr. Shaw and asked when the administration has a right to confront students about what is posted on their Internet sites. He responded, "When you are linking a site to the school or a group is directly linked to the school and they are taking their smut and associating it to the values of the school. Most private schools have students sign a code of conduct. It's really an integrity issue."

As I interviewed Mr. Shaw, his concerns seemed reasonable and caring. Mr. Shaw had nothing to do with the letters being sent home, he said. He made a "blanket statement" to his classes about the dangers of MySpace and personally encouraged students who had shown good taste, but he did not directly reprimand or discipline anyone or speak to parents. This indirect approach worked well. "Six of the kids changed their MySpaces after I talked to the classes and had people think about what moral values you portray," he said.

When I asked what moved him to investigate, he said that a past speaker in our chapel services, the youth pastor from Church on the Way, had mentioned MySpace and the duty of a youth pastor to see what the youth are saying. He wasn't trying to be nosy, he said, he was just viewing out of concern. Mr. Shaw said he was shocked by the immoral photos and words he saw. "The rumors prepared me, yeah, but I didn't realize there'd be so many."

Although many students, especially girls, felt that he had violated their privacy and overstepped his obligations, he didn't think this was even an issue. "It's public domain. It's on the

Internet—anyone can see it. You shouldn't put anything [in] public that you'd be embarrassed about," he said.

What About Those Sexy Photos and the Random Ads?

Several of the photos he described as borderline child pornography. He also saw that a former student's MySpace had an advertisement with an indecent picture. Companies can advertise on

TEEN AND YOUNG ADULT ATTITUDES ON SENDING OR POSTING SEXUALLY SUGGESTIVE CONTENT

Teens | Young Adults

Say it can have serious negative consequences
75%
71%

Have sent or posted sexually suggestive e-mails or texts
39%
59%

Have sent or posted nude or semi-nude images of themselves
20%
33%

Taken from: National Campaign to Prevent Teen and Unplanned Pregnancy and CosmoGirl.com, "Sex and Tech: Results from a Survey of Teens and Young Adults," thenationalcampaign.org, December 10, 2008.

any MySpace, making it seem that the MySpace owner is endorsing the advertisement even though he or she has no say in it. "Is it really your space?" asked Mr. Shaw.

It is true that no one regulates the content on minors' MySpaces—in fact, many people lie about their age on MySpace. It is also true that anyone can view what is posted, from pornographic pictures to blogs about weekend drug experimentation to personal journal entries about depression. When MySpace owners realize how many people have viewed their page, they must consider that some of them could be men with dangerous intentions. When I have looked at MySpace, I have seen pictures of younger girls licking their fingers with seductive expressions or pulling on their shirts to show almost everything, and I am afraid for them. I love some of these girls [like] my kid sisters— they shouldn't even know about the things their poses suggest! It's not so much that I think they will meet some rapist in an alley—I have confidence in their intelligence—but I am sad that this exploitation is their idea of "fun." I believe that most of the teenagers who have provocative or controversial MySpaces don't realize their photos and blogs may be viewed by teachers, grandparents, prowling sex offenders—anyone. I think that when teens are alone in front of the computer, they tend to be more reckless than they normally are—those "social norms" that normally give people self-control aren't there and they "let loose."

However, most of my friends do not have scandalous MySpaces. Sometimes I look at them, but I usually end up bored (reading a profile for a close friend is about as interesting as filling out the personal information sheet on the SATs) or depressed that there are no pictures of me. The school newspaper might even get a MySpace if the staff pushes it enough. What is that? A newspaper can't take raunchy pictures of itself . . . it can't even have friends! My friends have joked that they will make me a MySpace and "be" me, but I made them promise not to. Everyone already sees me as "awful judgmental Selina who hates MySpace." I don't want them to think I'm a total hypocrite also.

I don't see a reason for me to have a MySpace. However, I strongly support students' rights to have them. Schools may warn parents, but if they go any further and threaten to damage a student's academic record for content on a personal Web page, I believe that these schools have violated individual rights. Attorney Mark Goodman, who specializes in student free speech, said that in California private schools can't discipline students purely based on the things they say or write, even if schools disagree with them or even if the code of conduct says otherwise. Perhaps MySpace is addicting and unwise, but schools are meant to teach and guide, not force morality or personal decisions. Students should not let anyone control their MySpace, but they should be aware of the risks and create their profiles in a responsible, thoughtful way. If I had a MySpace, it would seem obvious to me that the surreal mindset, invasive advertisements and unrestrained viewers kept the page from being my space, but it's not my school's space either.

"[Restricting access to social networks] exaggerates the . . . difference in access to the defining cultural experiences that take place around technology today."

Banning Social Networks Would Be Counterproductive

Wade Roush

In the following viewpoint, Wade Roush asserts that the Deleting Online Predators Act of 2006, an unpassed bill intended to prohibit social networks at federally funded libraries and schools, would deprive disadvantaged youths of access to dozens of online communities, which are vital to teen culture. The bill covers any site with profile and chatting capabilities, including those for educational use and media sharing, the author contends. Moreover, such legislation would drive social networks underground, making it more difficult for guardians and authorities to monitor, he claims. Based in San Francisco, California, Roush is a technology and digital media journalist.

The social-networking site MySpace has 95 million registered users [in 2006]. If it were a country, it would be the 12th largest in the world (ranking between Mexico and the Philippines). But under a bill designed to combat sexual predators on the

Wade Roush, "The Moral Panic Over Social-Networking Sites," *Technology Review*, August 7, 2006. Copyright © 2006 by Technology Review, Inc. All rights reserved. Reproduced by permission.

Internet, MySpace and similar sites would become countries that young people can't visit—at least not using computers at schools or libraries.

The Deleting Online Predators Act (DOPA), introduced in the U.S. House of Representatives in May [2006] by [Pennsylvania Republican] Michael Fitzpatrick . . . was passed by a vote of 410 to 15 on July 26. It requires, with few exemptions, that facilities receiving federal aid block minors from accessing commercial social-networking sites and chat rooms, where they might encounter adults seeking sexual contact.

The bill has now moved on to the Senate. Critics from the worlds of educational technology and media studies say they're alarmed that the legislation has advanced this far. They warn that it would do little to stop sexual predators, but [it] would deprive youth from poor areas of their only access to the online communities that are an increasingly critical part of teen culture. To these critics, the act is an election-year stunt designed to make any member of Congress who opposes it look "soft" on sexual predators.

It's a "monumentally ill-considered piece of legislation" that "by any rational measure" should never have left the House, says Henry Jenkins, professor of literature and director of the Comparative Media Studies Program at MIT [Massachusetts Institute of Technology]. Jenkins believes the act plays on parents' lack of understanding, and their resulting fears, about their kids' activities on the Internet. "But the price of standing up to that fear may be too high for liberal Democrats," he says.

If the Senate approves a similar bill and the legislation reaches President [George W.] Bush's desk, the price to young people will be even higher, say Jenkins and other critics. "If it would actually prevent predation, I would be fine with it," says Danah Boyd—a PhD candidate in the School of Information Management Sciences at the University of California, Berkeley—who is considered one of the leading scholarly authorities on social-networking sites. "But it's not going to help at all. Out of 300,000

Representative Michael Fitzpatrick of Pennsylvania, right, introduced the Deleting Online Predators Act in 2006. Some characterized the proposed legislation as an election-year ploy to make political opponents appear "soft" on pedophiles. © AP Images/Pablo Martinez Monsivais.

child abductions every year, only 12 are by strangers. This is just going to stifle the social-networking industry and completely segment youth around economic status."

The Participation Gap

The impact on youth from economically disadvantaged families is what Jenkins worries about most. "Already, you have a gap between kids who have 10 minutes of Internet access a day at the public library and kids who have 24-hour-a-day access at home," he says. "Already, we have filters in libraries [required under the Children's Internet Protection Act of 2001] blocking access to much of the Internet. Now we're talking about adding even more restrictions. It exaggerates the 'participation gap'—not a technology gap, but a difference in access to the defining cultural experiences that take place around technology today."

Using Social Networks to Assert Identity

Emerging identity is an important aspect of early adolescent development, and in our existing digital culture children have an immense opportunity to explore their world, be creative, play with identity and experiment with different social mores. Using SNSs [social networking sites] is not only entertaining for children . . . it is also highly creative and allows them to assert their identity in a totally unique way, checking out what their friends think of their creative endeavours.

Barbie Clarke, "BFFE (Be Friends Forever): The Way in Which Young Adolescents Are Using Social Networking Sites to Maintain Friendship and Explore Identity," http://journal.webscience .org, March 2009.

Current Internet filters at schools and libraries—some aimed at pornography and obscene materials, some already targeting social-networking sites—have "a tremendous chilling effect on education," agrees Jeff Cooper, an educational-technology consultant and former high-school teacher in Portland [Oregon]. "The 'Just Say No' philosophy has never worked," Cooper says. "You're lumping all social networking into the negative basket, and not giving kids any alternative. But there is so much good stuff online that nobody ever talks about."

Indeed, while it might be easy to agree that teens shouldn't be wasting time on MySpace or other social-networking sites while they're at school, DOPA would cover any site that allows networking and chatting. As one example, Cooper points to TappedIn .org, a social-networking and professional-development site for teachers. Students often use personal and public "rooms" on the site as part of virtual classroom activities. "It allows teachers to bring their students online in a very safe and secure environment," explains Cooper. "My concern isn't really that MySpace won't be accessible from schools, but that other sites like TappedIn will be banned."

DOPA supporters frequently cite a 2000 report about online sexual victimization funded by the National Center for Missing & Exploited Children, which concluded that one fifth of children have been sexually solicited in chat rooms, by instant message, or by e-mail. But in fact, as Boyd and other opponents point out, the same report states that most solicitations come from other young people—only 4 percent are from adults over 25—and that most kids deal with these solicitations simply by not answering or logging off. "To clamp down on a bunch of new networking sites really doesn't do anything" to stop sexual predators, says Cooper. "You might as well shut off the Internet entirely."

Opponents of DOPA misunderstand the bill, says Jeff Urbanchuck, a press officer for Representative Fitzpatrick. He says it is intended only to reduce the risk to teens from one particular category of websites—those where members can create online profiles and fill them with personal details, including e-mail or instant-messaging addresses, that help predators contact them. Critics are "extending beyond the MySpaces and Facebooks and arguing that the technology of social networking is so pervasive now that the Internet is going to become one big social-networking site," Urbanchuck says. "But the objective of the bill is to deal with the growing threat of online predators on specific sites that allow profiles. We want to tailor the bill to those sites."

Even banning access just to sites that allow profiles, however, would affect scores of educational, community, and media-sharing sites, including sites as popular as Flickr and as specialized as TappedIn. And in the longer term, predicts Boyd, the law would simply drive teen networking underground, where it would be more difficult for adults to monitor. "They'll be moving from site to site with a level of ephemerality that no one can keep up with," she says. "Not the cops—not even the designers of the technology."

"Cyberbullying is occurring both within the school environment and off-campus."

Laws Against Cyberbullying Are Necessary to Protect Young People

Nancy Willard

Nancy Willard is executive director of the Center for Safe and Responsible Internet Use and author of Cyberbullying and Cyberthreats: Responding to the Challenge of Online Social Aggression, Threats, and Distress. *In the following viewpoint, Willard contends that legislation should enable schools to respond to cyberbullying at levels that prevent the failure to act, violence, and suicide. School officials should be allowed to ensure the removal of harmful material online, and cyberbullying should be added to the list of already prohibited behaviors. Also, the legal standard that permits school officials to address off-campus harassment that causes, or threatens to cause, school disruption or interference with student safety should be incorporated into legislation and school policies, the author maintains.*

Nancy Willard, "Cyberbullying Legislation and School Policies: Where Are the Boundaries of the 'Schoolhouse Gate' in the New Virtual World?," Center for Safe and Responsible Internet Use, March 2007. Copyright © 2007 by Nancy Willard/Center for Safe and Responsible Internet Use. All rights reserved. Reproduced by permission.

L egislation is pending in a number of states to address the concern of cyberbullying. Many school districts are also adopting policies to address cyberbullying. This [viewpoint] will address key issues related to such legislation and policies.

Cyberbullying is being cruel to others by sending or posting harmful material or engaging in other forms of social cruelty using the Internet or other digital technologies. It has various forms, including direct harassment and indirect activities that are intended to damage the reputation or interfere with the relationships of the student targeted, such as posting harmful material, impersonating the person, disseminating personal information or images, or activities that result in exclusion.

Key Points to Consider

- Schools must address instances of cyberbullying occurring through use of the district Internet system or use of personal digital devices, such as cell phones, digital cameras, personal computers, and PDAs [personal digital assistant], while on campus.

- Some cyberbullying activities occurring off-campus are causing significant emotional harm to students. When students are emotionally harmed they may present a danger to themselves and to others. If school officials fail to effectively respond to these situations when they are at the "harmful speech" level, there is a risk that they will eventually have to respond at the "school failure," "school violence," or "student suicide" level.

- The legal standard enunciated by the courts governing when school officials can respond to off-campus online harmful speech is that school officials may impose formal discipline only when such speech causes, or threatens to cause, substantial and material disruption at school or interference with rights of students to be secure (*Tinker* standard).[1] The *Tinker* standard reflects an appropriate balance between student free speech rights and the school interests in en-suring student safety. It is strongly recommended that the *Tinker* standard be specifically incorporated into the legis-lation. [Sample] language is set forth below.

• It is further strongly recommended that school districts incorporate prevention and education strategies into safe school plans to address cyberbullying and related online risks and that the planning activities involve school employ-ees, law enforcement, community organizations, parents, and students. This may be accomplished through an amend-ment to a state statute addressing safe schools planning.

Cyberbullying Background

Cyberbullying is occurring both within the school environ-ment and off-campus. Sometimes students are using the district Internet system—during school, during after-school activities, or at home if the district has a laptop program or allows stu-dents to access the district system from home. Students may also use personal digital devices while at school, such as cell phones, digital cameras, PDAs, and personal computers . . . to engage in cyberbullying. In increasing numbers, students are bringing personal digital devices to school with the expectation that these devices will be used in the classroom for instructional activi-ties. Misuse of the district Internet system and personal digital devices on campus is clearly a concern that must be addressed by schools.

More frequently, students are engaging in the cyberbullying activities off-campus—but the harmful impact is being felt at school. There was a report of a school murder in Japan that was associated with cyberbullying. There are many emerging reports of school fights and other altercations, as well as reports of stu-dents who are so significantly emotionally harmed that they are avoiding school, forced [to] change schools, or are simply fail-ing. Also, there are increasing reports of youth suicide associated with cyberbullying.

STUDENTS AGES 12 TO 18 WHO REPORTED BULLYING AT SCHOOL AND CYBERBULLYING ANYWHERE, 2007

At school   Anywhere

Made fun of, called names, or insulted
21%

Subject of rumors
18%

Threatened with harm
6%

Pushed, shoved, tripped, or spit on
11%

Tried to make do things did not want to do
4%

Excluded from activities on purpose
5%

Property destroyed on purpose
4%

Hurtful information on Internet
2%

Unwanted contact on Internet
2%

Taken from: US Department of Justice, Bureau of Justice Statistics, School Crime Supplement (SCS) to the National Crime Victimization Survey, 2007.

It is necessary to understand that while the harmful online speech or interactions have been occurring off-campus, personal interactions between the bully [or bullies] and [the target/s] are occurring at school. It is this combination of online harm and on-campus interactions that presents significant concerns and risks for the safety of the students.

Because the original harm is being inflicted off-campus, responding to the harmful speech necessarily raises questions about the ability and responsibility of school officials to address this concern, as well as issues related to the free speech rights of students.

The following are some examples of cyberbullying and its possible impact at school:

> Some high school students created a "We hate Ashley" profile on a popular social networking profile. On this "slam book" profile, they have posted cruel and vicious comments about Ashley. They invite students to send Ashley email messages telling her how ugly she is and how no one likes her.
>
> Three students were involved in a school altercation. One was African American. Two were Caucasian. The principal addressed the situation and thought it had been resolved. Shortly thereafter, the two Caucasian students created a threatening racist profile on a social networking site. This site contained references to dragging African-American people behind cars and lynchings. Other students at school linked to the profile. The African-American student found out about the site and has told the Black Student Union.

In the first incident, there is clearly a significant risk that Ashley will have difficulties in school, resulting in school failure and avoidance. Further, she could respond by attacking the bullies at school or by committing suicide. In the second incident, there is a significant risk of school violence, as well as the perception among African-American students that the school is not safe for them.

Legal Background

When students are using the district Internet system, the district may govern student speech under standards enunciated in *Hazelwood School District v. Kuhlmeier*. The *Hazelwood* standard allows schools to impose educationally based restrictions on student speech. . . . Schools should be able to also impose *Hazelwood* standards whenever students are using such devices in the classroom for instructional activities. However, it is clear that schools can require that all on-campus use of these personal digital devices be covered by the district's policy against bullying and harassment.

Several courts have ruled on cases involving off-campus, on-line, harmful speech. The legal standard these courts applied was the *Tinker* standard. Under the *Tinker* standard, school officials may only respond with formal discipline in cases where the off-campus speech causes, or threatens to cause, a substantial and material disruption at school or interference with the rights of students to be secure. In most of these cases, the courts found that impact of the off-campus online speech did not meet the *Tinker* standard.

The application of the *Tinker* standard to off-campus student cyberbullying cases represents an appropriate balance between student free speech rights and the safety and security interests of schools. However, the imposition of a formal disciplinary response, such as suspension, will certainly be insufficient in and of itself to resolve these incidents. It is essential to ensure that harmful material is removed, the harmful activities cease, and retaliation by the student or by others at the student's request does not occur.

Additionally, if there is a question about the appropriateness of a formal disciplinary response under the *Tinker* standard, there should be nothing to prevent a school official from seeking to resolve the concern informally. The most effective response is to provide the parents of the cyberbully with a downloaded copy of the harmful online material and advise the parents of their

Students are increasingly bringing mobile devices to school expecting to use them for instruction, but instead are using them to engage in cyberbullying. © AP Images/Reed Hoffmann.

potential personal liability if they do not take proactive steps to ensure the harmful activities cease. It is preferable for school officials to seek to intervene informally, rather than to wait until such time that the standard of "substantial disruption or threat thereof" has materialized.

It should be recognized that the question of what standard should be applied to off-campus speech is an issue that is currently under consideration by the Supreme Court in the case of *Morse v. Frederick*. As of the writing of this document, this case has not yet been decided. [On June 25, 2007, the Supreme Court ruled that speech may be suppressed at school-oriented events.] However, the brief submitted by the ACLU [American Civil Liberties Union] for the petitioner in this case strongly urged the adoption of the *Tinker* standard for off-campus speech. Some [sample] comments:

> The Court [in *Tinker*] acknowledged the "special characteristics of the school environment" by permitting school officials to prohibit student speech if that speech would "substantially interfere with the work of the school or impinge upon the rights of other students."
>
> *Tinker* appropriately recognized that school officials have a duty to maintain an environment in which teachers can teach and students can learn.

A bill to address cyberbullying that has been signed into law in Arkansas, HB 1072, fully incorporated the *Tinker* standard and further provided legislative guidelines on the kinds of activities that were considered to meet the standard of "substantial disruption." This legislation provides an excellent model. However, it is likely not necessary to specifically include examples of what kinds of activities constitute "substantial disruption." If such examples are included, they should be prefaced by language that states: "including, but not limited to." . . .

Recommendations for Legislation and Policies

The following are three key recommendations for legislation and school policies to effectively address cyberbullying:

- State statutes and school policies directed at cyberbullying must specifically allow school officials to respond to instances of off-campus online speech that meets the *Tinker* standard, as well as address the use of the district Internet system and any personal digital devices used on campus. Two critical components of such legislation or policies are:

> Addition of cyberbullying [to] the list of prohibited actions. The best way to do this is to simply indicate that cyberbullying encompasses any of the already prohibited actions—such as bullying, discrimination, harassment, intimidation—accomplished through electronic means.
>
> Expansion of the description of the extent of authority to include any use of the district Internet system and on-campus use of personal digital devices and to include off-campus behavior that meets the *Tinker* standard. An example is the following language: "Any act that takes place on or immediately adjacent to school grounds, at any school-sponsored activity, on school-provided transportation or at any official school bus stop, use of the district Internet system, use of a personal digital device on campus, or off-campus activities that cause or threaten to cause a substantial and material disruption at school or interference with the rights of students to be secure."

- Most districts and schools have developed safe-schools plans in compliance with the No Child Left Behind Act. These plans address a full range of safety issues, including prevention. Effective planning involves teachers, administrators, students, parents, law enforcement, and community representatives. Legislation could either require or recommend that districts and schools incorporate cyberbullying into their safe-schools plans, which would be an effective way to more effectively address the concern of cyberbullying. Even without such legislation, school districts are encouraged to approach the concern of cyberbullying in the context of safe schools planning. . . .

• Additionally, given that there are other areas of youth risk online that could also directly impact schools, and clearly are impacting youth well-being, consideration should be given to including language in such legislation that will expand the safe-schools planning activities to address a wider range of youth risk online issues. The most significant additional issues of concern include:

> Unsafe online communities that are promoting cutting, anorexia, and suicide.
>
> Dangerous groups, including hate groups and gangs.
>
> Risky online sexual activities that range from posting sexually provocative material, to arranging for sexual "hookups," to involvement with online sexual predators.

Note

1. In *Tinker v. Des Moines* the Supreme Court decided that the First Amendment applied to public schools. It further found that in order for administrators to restrict speech they must be able to show that the speech or action would "substantially interfere with the requirements of appropriate discipline in the operation of the school."

| "States' efforts . . . have done little to resolve [instances] when threatening or unruly behavior trumps freedom of speech."

Laws Against Cyberbullying May Infringe on Free Speech

Alex Johnson

In the following viewpoint, Alex Johnson contends that cyberbullying policies raise concerns about the constitutional rights of young people and continue to divide the courts. In school districts nationwide, inexperienced local officials grapple with the task of protecting some students from online harassment and intimidation while preserving the free speech rights of others, he states. Furthermore, legal experts warn that such state and local laws violate the First Amendment by suppressing youth expression that takes place off-campus, Johnson maintains. The author coordinates news and interactive projects for NBC News and its affiliates, MSNBC and NBC News Channel.

A very Doninger has put off going to college so she can volunteer with AmeriCorps—at least when she's not in court. Doninger, 18, graduated from Lewis Mills High School in

Alex Johnson, "Rules to Curb Bullying Online Raise Concerns," MSNBC.COM, January 23, 2009. Copyright © 2009 by MSNBC Interactive News, LLC. Reproduced with permission of MSNBC Interactive News.

Burlington [Connecticut] last June [in 2008], but she has not left it behind. She is at the center of a landmark free-speech case, stemming from her days at the school, that appears headed for the Supreme Court.

Doninger was a star student at Mills, and in 2007 she wanted to run for senior class secretary, a position that included the honor of speaking at her graduation ceremony.

But Karissa Niehoff, the school's principal, rejected Doninger's candidacy over a personal blog entry Doninger posted from her home computer. In the posting, Doninger reported—inaccurately, it turned out—that a school event she had helped organize had been canceled. She blamed "douchebags in central office" for the supposed cancellation and reported that a flood of complaints had "pissed off" the school district's superintendent.

Doninger ran as a write-in candidate and won, only to be barred from taking office. That led her mother to sue the school district on her behalf. The Doningers lost this month [January 2009] in U.S. District Court; their attorney promised to appeal the decision all the way to the Supreme Court.

To Doninger, the case hinges on her First Amendment right to freedom of expression.

"I think that it's really important for students to stand up for their rights, because if we don't maintain democracy on the lowest levels, we'll never be able to maintain [it] on the highest levels," she said.

But to school officials, Doninger is a cyberbully whose writings threatened to disrupt operations at the school.

"When kids are in a position of privilege, there are certain standards of behavior we expect them to uphold," Niehoff said. "Our position stands for respect. We're just hoping kids appreciate the seriousness of any communication over the Internet."

Suicide Sparks a National Debate

Doninger's case, which runs contrary to the student-as-victim storyline typical of cyberbullying cases, illustrates the difficulty legislators and authorities are encountering as they try to rein in what experts say is an increasingly common and virulent form of harassment.

Connecticut does not have a law against cyberbullying, defined by the National Crime Prevention Council as the use [of] "the Internet, cell phones, or other devices . . . to send or post text or images intended to hurt or embarrass another person." The state has an anti-bullying statute on the books, but it says nothing about the Internet and electronic communications, and it addresses only situations in which students are the victims.

But states' efforts to bring some clarity to the realm of new communications technologies like blogs, instant messages and e-mail have done little to resolve [instances] when threatening or unruly behavior trumps freedom of speech, said Jeffrey Shaman, a First Amendment scholar at the DePaul University College of Law in Chicago.

"Prohibiting the libelous speech, prohibiting [and] regulating true threats, regulating harassment under certain circumstances—these laws need to be more precisely defined," he said.

The issue of cyberbullying became the focus of a national debate last year [2008], after Lori Drew, 49, was prosecuted in connection with the suicide of 13-year-old Megan Meier of Dardenne Prairie [Missouri], in October 2006.

Believing Megan had spread rumors about her own daughter, Drew and an employee of her small business assumed a false identity, that of a 16-year-old boy. After winning Megan's trust, they began sending her venomous messages through her MySpace account.

"You are a bad person and everybody hates you," said the last message sent to Megan from the fake account, according to court documents. "Have a [expletive] rest of your life. The world would be a better place without you."

Later that day, Megan was found hanging from her neck in a closet; she died the next day.

Local prosecutors concluded that there was no law addressing Drew's behavior, and they declined to press charges. But in May [2008], a federal grand jury in Los Angeles, where MySpace .com has its headquarters, indicted Drew on charges of accessing protected computers without authorization to obtain information to inflict emotional distress—in other words, violating MySpace's terms of use by faking an identity.

Drew was convicted of three misdemeanor violations of the federal Computer Fraud and Abuse Act and faces a maximum of three years in prison when she is sentenced in April [2009].[1]

The case was closely followed in Internet forums and blogs, in which many commentators complained that Drew was being prosecuted for ignoring the fine print of her MySpace account, not for a role in driving Megan to kill herself. And in its wake, a national movement to clamp down on cyberbullying—psychological abuse by and of children through the Internet—was born.

Biggest Online Threat to Children?

According to the members of a task force appointed to assess protections for children on the Internet, more needs to be done.

In a report last month [December 2008], the task force— appointed by a coalition of 49 state attorneys general (a spokeswoman said Texas Attorney General Greg Abbott did not take part and did not endorse the findings)—concluded that while online sexual predation of minors generated more headlines, "bullying and harassment, most often by peers . . . [were] the most frequent threats that minors face."

The report, which was directed by the Berkman Center for Internet & Society at Harvard University, cited 2007 research indicating that 1 in 6 American middle-school students had been the targets of cyberbullying, with effects ranging from depression

---

Lori Drew was accused of harassing one of her daughter's classmates by sending vicious messages to the girl via a phony MySpace page. The classmate eventually committed suicide. Drew was acquitted of all charges. © AP Images/Nick Ut.

to anxiety to "negative social views of themselves." Separate research last year by the U.S. Centers for Disease Control and Prevention found that as many as a third of all children had been the victims of online bullying.

Among numerous other technological and social recommendations, the task force called for law enforcement to allocate more resources for training, technology and enforcement to protect children from online bullies.

At least 35 states have enacted new laws or updated old laws to address bullying on the Internet. Some of those [laws] are general cyberstalking prohibitions that are not specifically targeted at schools, while others generally require local school districts to develop and enforce cyberbullying policies, as hundreds of districts across the nation have done already.

That leaves it up to local school officials—who may or may not be well versed in online etiquette or the twists of constitu-

Society Must Make Cyberbullying Unacceptable

The new technology, the internet, text messaging, all of these things offer a degree of anonymity that give courage to those who would never have the nerve to say such things openly. . . . Couple this sense of anonymity with a culture that has coarsened, a culture where one is liberated from decent behavior, and you have a recipe for this very thing. It must become a matter of unacceptable ill-manners on the part of the average computer user [to cyberbully]—be they adult, teen, or tween. The law is simply inadequate for dealing with this sort in any but the most ham-handed—and ultimately restrictive—fashion.

Timothy Birdnow, "Cyberbullying Law and the Moral Code," American Thinker, May 24, 2009.

tional law—to weigh the need to shield some students from harassment against the rights of others to speak freely. And it has led to a patchwork approach to the problem.

The school district in Duluth [Minnesota], for instance, monitors all e-mail sent using students' district accounts under what it calls the Internet Safety Program. It also offers parents monitoring equipment so they can keep track of their children's social networking activities at home.

If a student's e-mail message includes "bullying-type words or inappropriate words in general, then we'll send that e-mail to a section where an administrator has to review it," said Keith Anderson, the district's coordinator of media technology.

In the Northside Independent School District in San Antonio, Texas, on the other hand, schools actively block social networking sites, among them MySpace and Facebook, said Joyce Stevens, the district's director of technology.

The policies usually go beyond addressing students who bully students. More and more, authorities are responding to online attacks by students on teachers and administrators, as in the case of Avery Doninger.

"The problem of young people targeting teachers and other school staff is one that appears to be growing," said Nancy Willard, director of the Center for Safe and Responsible Internet Use, a nonprofit group in Eugene [Oregon]. Such attacks can be anything from "just a comment that's negative about a teacher to really serious kinds of incidents."

Constitutional Doubts Linger

Most such laws and policies have been enacted only in the past year or so, making it difficult to gauge their effectiveness. Still, they do give school officials tools to work with, administrators say.

"As far as making it clear this is inappropriate and not going to be tolerated, it's nice to have language clearly stated in legislation and a potential policy in the future," said Pam Hedgpeth, superintendent of the Republic School District in Missouri, which passed a cyberbullying law last year [2008] in the wake of Megan Meier's death.

But legal experts say state laws and local policies are problematic, bumping up as they do against First Amendment protections of freedom of speech.

"Permitting school officials to restrict student speech in the digital media expands the authority of school officials to clamp down on juvenile expression in a way previously unthinkable," Mary-Rose Papandrea, a law professor at Boston College specializing in media law, wrote in the October [2008] edition of the *Florida Law Review*.

Papandrea zeroed in on a particularly contentious point for skeptics—the assumption that school administrators can punish students for what they write on their own time, away from school, a question that is at the heart of Avery Doninger's suit.

"Because digital speech is generally nowhere and everywhere at the same time," Papandrea wrote, "permitting school officials to restrict such speech simply because it is accessed on school grounds, because it is somehow directed to the school grounds, or because it was reasonably foreseeable that it would come to the attention of school officials gives schools far too much authority to restrict the speech of juveniles generally."

Little Guidance from the Courts

Courts remain divided over whether administrators' power to regulate students' online writings extends off campus, said David L. Hudson, a legal scholar for the First Amendment Center at Vanderbilt University in Nashville, [Tennessee].

"It will probably take a decision by the U.S. Supreme Court to provide the necessary guidance to resolve these thorny issues," Hudson concluded in a legal analysis for the center in August [2008].

Even Kentucky Attorney General Jack Conway, who supports his state's recently passed law requiring school officials to report cyberbullying to police, says: "I'll readily grant that this is a gray area. It's a tough area."

Judges who have ruled in the case of Avery Doninger wrestled with that question before ruling that school officials were justified in punishing her for her off-campus postings.

"The Supreme Court has yet to speak on the scope of a school's authority to regulate expression that, like Avery's, does not occur on school grounds or at a school-sponsored event," wrote a three-judge panel of the 2nd U.S. Circuit Court of Appeals in rejecting Doninger's initial appeal in May [2008].

Without such guidance, the panel said, it could rely only on case law that predates the spread of the Internet.

"Avery's post created a foreseeable risk of substantial disruption to the work and discipline of the school," they wrote, adding that under that test, the record "failed to show clearly that Avery's First Amendment rights were violated."

Doninger acknowledges that the posting was "not my finest moment."

"I've never been in trouble," she wrote in an essay accompanying her college applications. "I am an engaged student, yet I did use an unsavory word."

But "I believe in democracy," she wrote. "I believe in the Constitution and the Bill of Rights. I believe that each citizen is responsible for participating in the maintenance of democracy by challenging government officials when they overreach.

"The principal accused me of failing to be a good citizen. I disagree. Apathy and passivity are poor citizenship."

Note

1. Drew's sentencing was postponed until July 2009, when the federal judge in the case overturned the guilty verdicts and acquitted Drew of the charges.

| "*Like a lot of people, I'd always accepted every friend request, never thinking it could be dangerous.*"

A College Student Discusses How Cyberbullying Threatened Her Education

Personal Narrative

Lynda Lopez

Lynda Lopez is a student at the University of Chicago and a graduate of Prosser Career Academy in Chicago. In the following viewpoint, Lopez provides an account of how cyberbullying jeopardized her scholarship and college education. After posting on Facebook that she was a finalist for two college scholarships, Lopez writes that an impersonator e-mailed rude messages to the scholarship organizations and death threats to her. It took authorities several months to help her identify the perpetrator, the author continues, who received a slap on the wrist from the court. Although ultimately awarded full tuition, Lopez reveals that she is now cautious of friend requests and does not trust Facebook with her privacy.

Lynda Lopez, "How a Cyberbully Almost Ruined My Life: Lynda Lopez, 19, on the Vicious E-mails and Death Threats That Nearly Sank Her College Plans—and How She Fought Back," *New York Times Upfront*, September 6, 2010, p. 29. Copyright © 2010 by Scholastic Inc. and the New York Times Company. Reprinted by permission of Scholastic Inc.

In October 2009, I learned that I was a finalist for a full scholarship to Carleton College in Northfield, Minnesota. When I got the news, I did what any teen today would do: I posted it on Facebook. The next day, I found out I was also a finalist for the Questbridge National College Match Scholarship. Before heading out to dinner and a movie with a friend, I updated my Facebook status with the good news.

But my festive mood that night was shattered by a call from the Posse Foundation, which was offering the scholarship to Carleton College.

"Lynda," said the woman at Posse, "we received your e-mail. It said you wanted to drop out of the program because the scholarship was a piece of crap."

I told her that the e-mail wasn't from me. When I got home, I had an e-mail from another foundation I had applied to: "Call us immediately," which I did.

"We received your insulting e-mail and our president is deeply upset," their representative told me.

The sender's e-mail address was nearly identical to mine. I explained that someone must be trying to sabotage my applications. The woman told me to write a statement to the president of the organization.

I quickly completed my statement and sent it to all the colleges and scholarships I had applied to. Then I checked my e-mail. There were 12 messages with the subject "I will kill you." One of them repeated the threat more than 50 times, along with obscenities about "stealing my scholarship."

No one else except my family would have known yet that I was a scholarship finalist, so I knew that whoever was behind this had to be on my list of Facebook friends. Like a lot of people, I'd always accepted every friend request, never thinking it could be dangerous.

At midnight, my mother and sister went with me to the police station. The officer seemed indifferent when I told him about the death threats. He said a detective would call in a few days.

But as weeks went by and I continued to receive death threats I became wary of everyone around me.

A Slap on the Wrist

It was early December [2009] when a detective finally called. By then, the impostor had also contacted Carleton College. This person could have jeopardized my college education.

They found the perpetrator in January [2010]: It was a girl I'd worked with at an old job; she was a senior at another high school and ultracompetitive. Although she wasn't arrested, she was charged with harassment by electronic communication—

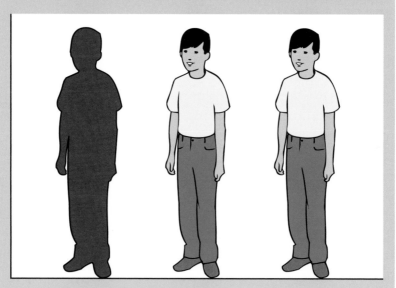

CYBERBULLIED KIDS WHO DON'T REPORT ABUSE

About one out of three children who are cyberbullied do not tell because they do not want their parents to restrict their Internet access.

Taken from: Stuart Wolpert, "Bullying of Teenagers Online Is Common, UCLA Psychologists Report," UCLA Newsroom, October 2, 2008. newsroom.ucla.edu.

a misdemeanor in Illinois punishable by up to six months in prison and a $1,500 fine.

A hearing took place in February [2010], and the court imposed a one-year supervision period, which means the girl can't have any unlawful contact with me for a year. She wasn't put on trial or convicted of any crime.

Illinois law states that electronic harassment becomes a felony only after the second offense. Although this girl had harassed and impersonated me more than once, her actions were considered a single offense under the law. She got off with a slap on the wrist.

Fortunately, the scholarship organizations had all believed my statement: I was ultimately awarded a full-tuition Questbridge scholarship to the University of Chicago.

But this ordeal has shaken my trust in social networking sites. I no longer accept friend requests from mere acquaintances, and Facebook's ever-changing privacy policies have left me concerned about who can see what on my profile.

My mission is to pursue a change in Illinois cyberbullying law. I hope that my voice and those of other victims will be heard and eventually lead to stricter laws. Maybe the state didn't want to ruin an 18-year-old's life because of one offense—even if she had been willing to ruin mine.

> *"Society must develop a new and more
> nuanced understanding of public and
> private life."*

Social Networks May Erode Young People's Privacy

Daniel J. Solove

Daniel J. Solove is a professor at the George Washington University Law School and author of The Future of Reputation: Gossip, Rumor, and Privacy on the Internet *and* Understanding Privacy. *By sharing personal and sensitive information on social networking sites, "Generation Google" is redrawing the line between the public and private, Solove argues in the following viewpoint. Widespread, instant access to "digital baggage" such as embarrassing videos and photographs, the author states, threaten the reputations of young people. And Facebook's recent practices have distributed names, images, and online behaviors without adequately informing users. Therefore, Solove suggests that appropriation and privacy laws in the United States must be overhauled to balance the right to privacy with the dissemination of public information.*

He has a name, but most people just know him as "the Star Wars Kid." In fact, he is known around the world by tens of

Daniel J. Solove, "The End of Privacy," *Scientific American*, vol. 299, no. 3, September 2008, pp. 100–106. Copyright © 2008 by Scientific American, Inc. All rights reserved. Reproduced by permission.

millions of people. Unfortunately, his notoriety is for one of the most embarrassing moments in his life.

In 2002, as a 15-year-old, the Star Wars Kid videotaped himself waving around a golf-ball retriever while pretending it was a light saber. Without the help of the expert choreographers working on the *Star Wars* movies, he stumbled around awkwardly in the video.

The video was found by some of the boy's tormentors, who uploaded it to an Internet video site. It became an instant hit with a multitude of fans. All across the blogosphere, people started mocking the boy, making fun of him for being pudgy, awkward and nerdy.

Several remixed videos of the Star Wars Kid started popping up, adorned with special effects. People edited the video to make the golf-ball retriever glow like a light saber. They added *Star Wars* music to the video. Others mashed it up with other movies. Dozens of embellished versions were created. The Star Wars Kid appeared in a video game and on the television shows *Family Guy* and *South Park*. It is one thing to be teased by classmates in school, but imagine being ridiculed by masses the world over. The teenager dropped out of school and had to seek counseling. What happened to the Star Wars Kid can happen to anyone, and it can happen in an instant. Today collecting personal information has become second nature. More and more people have cell phone cameras, digital audio recorders, Web cameras and other recording technologies that readily capture details about their lives.

For the first time in history nearly anybody can disseminate information around the world. People do not need to be famous enough to be interviewed by the mainstream media. With the Internet, anybody can reach a global audience.

Technology has led to a generational divide. On one side are high school and college students whose lives virtually revolve around social-networking sites and blogs. On the other side are their parents, for whom recollection of the past often remains locked in fading memories or, at best, in books, photographs and videos. For the current generation, the past is preserved on the Internet, potentially forever. And this change raises the question of how much privacy people can expect—or even desire—in an age of ubiquitous networking.

Generation Google

The number of young people using social-networking Web sites such as Facebook and MySpace is staggering. At most college campuses, more than 90 percent of students maintain their own sites. I call the people growing up today "Generation Google." For them, many fragments of personal information will reside on the Internet forever, accessible to this and future generations through a simple Google search.

That openness is both good and bad. People can now spread their ideas everywhere without reliance on publishers, broadcasters or other traditional gatekeepers. But that transformation also creates profound threats to privacy and reputations.

Copyright © 2010 Paul Zanetti, Australia, and PoliticalCartoons.com.

The *New York Times* is not likely to care about the latest gossip at Dubuque Senior High School or Oregon State University. Bloggers and others communicating online may care a great deal. For them, stories and rumors about friends, enemies, family members, bosses, co-workers and others are all prime fodder for Internet postings.

Before the Internet, gossip would spread by word of mouth and remain within the boundaries of that social circle. Private details would be confined to diaries and kept locked in a desk drawer. Social networking spawned by the Internet allows communities worldwide to revert to the close-knit culture of preindustrial society, in which nearly every member of a tribe or a farming hamlet knew everything about the neighbors. Except that now the "villagers" span the globe.

College students have begun to share salacious details about their schoolmates. A Web site called Juicy Campus serves as an electronic bulletin board that allows students nationwide to post anonymously and without verification a sordid array of tidbits about sex, drugs and drunkenness. Another site, Don't Date Him Girl, invites women to post complaints about the men they have dated, along with real names and actual photographs.

Social-networking sites and blogs are not the only threat to privacy. . . . Companies collect and use our personal information at every turn. Your credit-card company has a record of your purchases. If you shop online, merchants keep tabs on every item you have bought. Your Internet service provider has information about how you surf the Internet. Your cable company has data about which television shows you watch.

The government also compromises privacy by assembling vast databases that can be searched for suspicious patterns of behavior. The National Security Agency listens and examines the records of millions of telephone conversations. Other agencies analyze financial transactions. Thousands of government bodies at the federal and state level have records of personal information, chronicling births, marriages, employment, property ownership and more. The information is often stored in public records, making it readily accessible to anyone—and the trend toward more accessible personal data continues to grow as more records become electronic.

The Future of Reputation

Broad-based exposure of personal information diminishes the ability to protect reputation by shaping the image that is presented to others. Reputation plays an important role in society, and preserving private details of one's life is essential to it. We look to people's reputations to decide whether to make friends, go on a date, hire a new employee or undertake a prospective business deal.

Some would argue that the decline of privacy might allow people to be less inhibited and more honest. But when everybody's transgressions are exposed, people may not judge one another less harshly. Having your personal information may fail to improve my judgment of you. It may, in fact, increase the likelihood that I will hastily condemn you. Moreover, the loss of privacy might inhibit freedom. Elevated visibility that comes with living in a transparent online world means you may never overcome past mistakes.

People want to have the option of "starting over," of reinventing themselves throughout their lives. As American philosopher John Dewey once said, a person is not "something complete, perfect, [or] finished," but is "something moving, changing, discrete, and above all initiating instead of final." In the past, episodes of youthful experimentation and foolishness were eventually forgotten, giving us an opportunity to start anew, to change and to grow. But with so much information online, it is harder to make these moments forgettable. People must now live with the digital baggage of their pasts.

This openness means that the opportunities for members of Generation Google might be limited because of something they did years ago as wild teenagers. Their intimate secrets may be revealed by other people they know. Or they might become the unwitting victim of a false rumor. Like it or not, many people are beginning to get used to having a lot more of their personal information online.

What Is to Be Done?

Can we prevent a future in which so much information about people's private lives circulates beyond their control? Some technologists and legal scholars flatly say no. Privacy, they maintain, is just not compatible with a world in which information flows so freely. As Scott McNealy of Sun Microsystems once famously declared: "You already have zero privacy. Get over it." Countless books and articles have heralded the "end," "death" and "destruction" of privacy.

Those proclamations are wrongheaded at best. It is still possible to protect privacy, but doing so requires that we rethink outdated understandings of the concept. One such view holds that privacy requires total secrecy: once information is revealed to others, it is no longer private. This notion of privacy is unsuited to an online world. The generation of people growing up today understands privacy in a more nuanced way. They know that personal information is routinely shared with countless others, and they also know that they leave a trail of data wherever they go.

The more subtle understanding of privacy embraced by Generation Google recognizes that a person should retain some control over personal information that becomes publicly available. This generation wants a say in how private details of their lives are disseminated.

The issue of control over personal information came to the fore in 2006, when Facebook launched a feature called News Feeds, which sent a notice to people's friends registered with the service when their profile was changed or updated. But to the great surprise of those who run Facebook, many of its users reacted with outrage. Nearly 700,000 of them complained. At first

Those who engage in social networking and online shopping may be providing personal details that become part of their online reputation. © AP Images/Ben Margot.

blush, the outcry over News Feeds seems baffling. Many of the users who protested had profiles completely accessible to the public. So why did they think it was a privacy violation to alert their friends to changes in their profiles?

Instead of viewing privacy as secrets hidden away in a dark closet, they considered the issue as a matter of accessibility. They figured that most people would not scrutinize their profiles carefully enough to notice minor changes and updates. They could make changes inconspicuously. But Facebook's News Feeds made information more widely noticeable. The privacy objection, then, was not about secrecy; it was about accessibility.

In 2007 Facebook again encountered another privacy outcry when it launched an advertising system with two parts, called Social Ads and Beacon. With Social Ads, whenever users wrote something positive about a product or a movie, Facebook would use their names, images and words in advertisements sent to friends in the hope that an endorsement would induce other users to purchase a product more than an advertisement might.

With Beacon, Facebook made data-sharing deals with a variety of other commercial Web sites. If a person bought a movie ticket on Fandango or an item on another site, that information would pop up in that person's public profile.

Facebook rolled out these programs without adequately informing its users. People unwittingly found themselves shilling products on their friends' Web sites. And some people were shocked to see their private purchases on other Web sites suddenly displayed to the public as part of their profiles that appeared on the Facebook site.

The outcry and an ensuing online petition called for Facebook to reform its practices—a document that quickly attracted tens of thousands of signatures and that ultimately led to several changes. As witnessed in these instances, privacy does not always involve sharing of secrets. Facebook users did not want their identities used to endorse products with Social Ads. It is one thing to write about how much one enjoys a movie or CD; it is another to be used on a billboard to pitch products to others.

Changing the Law

Canada and most European countries have more stringent privacy statutes than the U.S., which has resisted enacting all-encompassing legislation. Privacy laws elsewhere recognize that revealing information to others does not extinguish one's right to privacy. Increasing accessibility of personal information, however, means that U.S. law also should begin recognizing the need to safeguard a degree of privacy in the public realm.

In some areas, U.S. law has a well-developed system of controlling information. Copyright recognizes strong rights for public information, protecting a wide range of works, from movies to software. Procuring copyright protection does not require locking a work of intellect behind closed doors. You can read a copyrighted magazine, make a duplicate for your own use and lend it to others. But you cannot do whatever you want: for instance, photocopying it from cover to cover or selling bootleg copies in the street. Copyright law tries to achieve a balance between freedom and control, even though it still must wrestle with the ongoing controversies in a digital age.

The closest U.S. privacy law comes to a legal doctrine akin to copyright is the appropriation tort, which prevents the use of someone else's name or likeness for financial benefit. Unfortunately, the law has developed in a way that is often ineffective against the type of privacy threats now cropping up. Copyright primarily functions as a form of property right, protecting works of self-expression, such as a song or painting. To cope with increased threats to privacy, the scope of the appropriation tort should be expanded. The broadening might actually embody the original early 20th-century interpretation of this principle of common law, which conceived of privacy as more than a means to protect property: "The right to withdraw from the public gaze at such times as a person may see fit . . . is embraced within the right of personal liberty," declared the Georgia Supreme Court in 1905. Today, however, the tort does not apply when a person's name or image appears in news, art, literature, or on social-networking sites. At the same time the appropriation tort protects against using someone's name or picture without consent to advertise products, it allows these representations to be used in a news story. This limitation is fairly significant. It means that the tort would rarely apply to Internet-related postings.

Any widening of the scope of the appropriation tort must be balanced against the competing need to allow legitimate news gathering and dissemination of public information. The tort should probably apply only when photographs and other personal information are used in ways that are not of public concern—a criterion that will inevitably be subject to ongoing judicial deliberation.

Appropriation is not the only common-law privacy tort that needs an overhaul to become more relevant in an era of networked digital communications. We already have many legal tools to protect privacy, but they are currently crippled by conceptions of privacy that prevent them from working effectively. A broader development of the law should take into account problematic uses of personal information illustrated by the Star Wars Kid or Facebook's Beacon service.

It would be best if these disputes could be resolved without recourse to the courts, but the broad reach of electronic networking will probably necessitate changes in common law. The threats to privacy are formidable, and people are starting to realize how strongly they regard privacy as a basic right. Toward this goal, society must develop a new and more nuanced understanding of public and private life—one that acknowledges that more personal information is going to be available yet also protects some choice over how that information is shared and distributed.

| "Many members of the tell-all generation are rethinking what it means to live out loud."

Young People Are More Protective of Their Privacy on Social Networks

Laura M. Holson

In the following viewpoint, Laura M. Holson writes that the "tell-all generation" is more discreet in what they reveal on social networking sites than other users. Seeking educational and career opportunities, users in their teens and twenties remove or refrain to post content that can compromise their digital reputations, she insists, showing more diligence than older adults. Additionally, Holson maintains that a growing number of young adults mistrust social networking sites with their privacy, sharing less and teaching others to keep more of their personal life offline. The author is an award-winning reporter for the New York Times *and covers communications and mobile technology.*

Laura M. Holson, "Tell-All Generation Learns to Keep Things Offline," *New York Times*, May 8, 2010. © 2010 The New York Times. All rights reserved. Used by permission and protected by the copyright laws of the United States. The printing, copying, redistribution, or retransmission of this content without express written permission is prohibited.

Min Liu, a 21-year-old liberal arts student at the New School in New York City, got a Facebook account at 17 and chronicled her college life in detail, from rooftop drinks with friends to dancing at a downtown club. Recently, though, she has had second thoughts.

Concerned about her career prospects, she asked a friend to take down a photograph of her drinking and wearing a tight dress. When the woman overseeing her internship asked to join her Facebook circle, Ms. Liu agreed, but limited access to her Facebook page. "I want people to take me seriously," she said.

The conventional wisdom suggests that everyone under 30 is comfortable revealing every facet of their lives online, from their favorite pizza to most frequent sexual partners. But many members of the tell-all generation are rethinking what it means to live out loud.

While participation in social networks is still strong, a survey released last month [April 2010] by the University of California, Berkeley, found that more than half the young adults questioned had become more concerned about privacy than they were five years ago—mirroring the number of people their parent's age or older with that worry.

More Diligence and Mistrust

They are more diligent than older adults, however, in trying to protect themselves. In a new study to be released this month, the Pew Internet Project has found that people in their 20s exert more control over their digital reputations than older adults, more vigorously deleting unwanted posts and limiting information about themselves. "Social networking requires vigilance, not only in what you post, but what your friends post about you," said Mary Madden, a senior research specialist who oversaw the study by Pew, which examines online behavior. "Now you are responsible for everything."

The erosion of privacy has become a pressing issue among active users of social networks. Last week [May 2010], Facebook scrambled to fix a security breach that allowed users to see their friends' supposedly private information, including personal chats.

Sam Jackson, a junior at Yale who started a blog when he was 15 and who has been an intern at Google, said he had learned not to trust any social network to keep his information private. "If I go back and look, there are things four years ago I would not say today," he said. "I am much more self-censoring. I'll try to be honest and forthright, but I am conscious now who I am talking to."

He has learned to live out loud mostly by trial and error and has come up with his own theory: concentric layers of sharing.

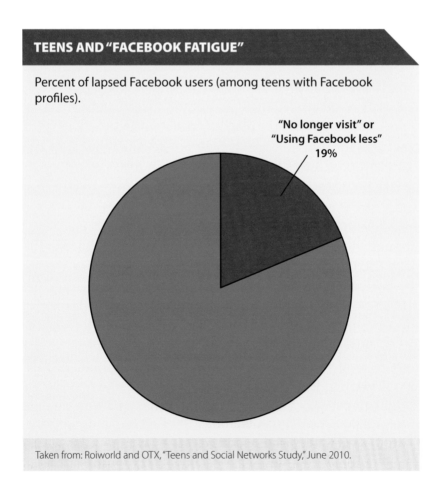

TEENS AND "FACEBOOK FATIGUE"

Percent of lapsed Facebook users (among teens with Facebook profiles).

"No longer visit" or "Using Facebook less" 19%

Taken from: Roiworld and OTX, "Teens and Social Networks Study," June 2010.

His Facebook account, which he has had since 2005, is strictly personal. "I don't want people to know what my movie rentals are," he said. "If I am sharing something, I want to know what's being shared with others."

Mistrust of the intentions of social sites appears to be pervasive. In its telephone survey of 1,000 people, the Berkeley Center for Law and Technology at the University of California found that 88 percent of the 18- to 24-year-olds it surveyed last July [2009] said there should be a law that requires Web sites to delete stored information. And 62 percent said they wanted a law that gave people the right to know everything a Web site knows about them.

That mistrust is translating into action. In the Pew study, to be released shortly, researchers interviewed 2,253 adults late last summer [2009] and found that people ages 18 to 29 were more apt to monitor privacy settings than older adults are, and they more often delete comments or remove their names from photos so they cannot be identified. Younger teenagers were not included in these studies, and they may not have the same privacy concerns. But anecdotal evidence suggests that many of them have not had enough experience to understand the downside to oversharing.

Elliot Schrage, who oversees Facebook's global communications and public policy strategy, said it was a good thing that young people are thinking about what they put online. "We are not forcing anyone to use it," he said of Facebook. But at the same time, companies like Facebook have a financial incentive to get friends to share as much as possible. That's because the more personal the information that Facebook collects, the more valuable the site is to advertisers, who can mine it to serve up more targeted ads.

Two weeks ago [in April 2010], Senator Charles E. Schumer, Democrat of New York, petitioned the Federal Trade Commission to review the privacy policies of social networks to make sure consumers are not being deliberately confused or misled.

The action was sparked by a recent change to Facebook's settings that forced its more than 400 million users to choose to "opt out" of sharing private information with third-party Web sites instead of "opt in," a move which confounded many of them.

Mr. Schrage of Facebook said, "We try diligently to get people to understand the changes."

Teaching One Another

But in many cases, young adults are teaching one another about privacy.

Ms. Liu is not just policing her own behavior, but her sister's, too. Ms. Liu sent a text message to her 17-year-old sibling warning her to take down a photo of a guy sitting on her sister's lap. Why? Her sister wants to audition for [the television series] *Glee*, and Ms. Liu didn't want the show's producers to see it. Besides, what if her sister became a celebrity? "It conjures up an image where if you became famous anyone could pull up a picture and send it to [celebrity gossip media source] TMZ," Ms. Liu said.

Andrew Klemperer, a 20-year-old at Georgetown University, said it was a classmate who warned him about the implications of the recent Facebook change—through a status update on (where else?) Facebook. Now he is more diligent in monitoring privacy settings and apt to warn others, too.

Helen Nissenbaum, a professor of culture, media and communication at New York University and author of *Privacy in Context*, a book about information-sharing in the digital age, said teenagers were naturally protective of their privacy as they navigate the path to adulthood, and the frequency with which companies change privacy rules has taught them to be wary.

That was the experience of Kanupriya Tewari, a 19-year-old pre-med student at Tufts University. Recently she sought to limit the information a friend could see on Facebook but found the

According to one study, younger people are more likely than older people to monitor their privacy setting in online forums and to delete unflattering material. © AP Images/Jack Dempsey.

process cumbersome. "I spent like an hour trying to figure out how to limit my profile, and I couldn't," she said. She gave up because she had chemistry homework to do, but vowed to figure . . . out [her privacy settings] after finals.

"I don't think they would look out for me," she said. "I have to look out for me."

> "The Commission is committed to
> protecting all consumers in the digital
> environment, especially . . . teens, who
> are particularly vulnerable to threats."

The Federal Trade Commission Protects the Privacy of Teens on Social Networks

Jessica Rich

Jessica Rich is the deputy director of the Bureau of Consumer Protection at the Federal Trade Commission (FTC). In the following testimony to a Senate subcommittee, Rich states that the FTC works to protect adolescents against privacy and safety risks online, especially risks posed by social networks and mobile devices. According to her, the commission educates young users about these sites and technologies—by partnering with schools, community groups, and law enforcement—and helps to evaluate the parental controls, blocking and filtering software, and other industry efforts. Rich also maintains that the FTC has brought action against social networks that failed to comply with the federal Internet law protecting children thirteen and younger and continues to review the law's enforcement and effectiveness.

Jessica Rich, "Prepared Statement of the Federal Trade Commission, 'Protecting Youths in an Online World,'" Federal Trade Commission, July 15, 2010.

Teens are heavy users of digital technology and new media applications including social networking, mobile devices, instant messaging, and file-sharing. Indeed, a 2007 study found that over 90 percent of kids between the ages of 12 and 17 spend time online. The online world has changed how teens learn, socialize, and are entertained. In many ways, the experiences teens have online are positive—they use the Internet to socialize with their peers, to learn more about topics that interest them, and to express themselves.

But teens also face unique challenges online. For example, research shows that teens tend to be more impulsive than adults and that they may not think as clearly as adults about the consequences of what they do. As a result, they may voluntarily disclose more information online than they should. On social networking sites, young people may share personal details that leave them vulnerable to identity theft. They may also share details that could adversely affect their potential employment or college admissions. Teens also sometimes "sext" . . . their peers—send text messages and images with sexual content—without considering the potential legal consequences and harm to their reputations. According to one recent study, 4 percent of cell phone owners aged 12 to 17 have sent sexually suggestive images of themselves by phone, while 15 percent have received "sexts" containing images of someone they know. In addition, bullies or predators— most often teens' own peers—may try to take advantage of adolescents on the Internet. About one-third of all teens online have reported experiencing some kind of online harassment, including cyberbullying.

Despite teens' sharing and use of personal information in the digital world, there is data that suggests teens are concerned about their online privacy. For example, one study of teens and privacy found that teens engage in a variety of techniques to obscure or conceal their real location or personal details on social networking sites. The [Federal Trade] Commission [FTC] seeks to address these privacy concerns—as well as parents' concerns about their teens' online behavior and interactions—through education, policy development, and law enforcement, as discussed further below.

Consumer Education

The FTC has launched a number of education initiatives designed to encourage consumers of all ages to use the Internet safely and responsibly. The commission's online safety portal, OnGuardOnline.gov, developed in partnership with other federal agencies, provides practical information in a variety of formats—including articles, games, quizzes, and videos—to help people guard against Internet fraud, secure their computers, and protect their personal information. The commission's booklet *Net Cetera: Chatting With Kids About Being Online* is the most recent addition to the OnGuardOnline.gov consumer education campaign. This guide provides practical tips on how parents, teachers, and other trusted adults can help children of all ages, including teens and pre-teens, reduce the risks of inappropriate conduct, contact, and content that come with living life online.

Net Cetera focuses on the importance of communicating with children about issues ranging from cyberbullying to sexting, social networking, mobile phone use, and online privacy. It provides specific advice to parents about talking to their children about each of these topics. For example, on the subject of sexting, it discusses the risks sexting poses to kids' reputations and friendships—as well as possible legal consequences if kids create, forward, or save these kinds of messages—and gives parents straightforward advice: "Tell your kids not to do it." With respect to cyberbullying, *Net Cetera* advises parents to talk with their kids about online behavior and about any messages or images that make them feel threatened or hurt. The guide advises parents to work with a child who is being bullied by helping them to not react, save the evidence, and block or delete the bully.

The commission has partnered with schools, community groups, and local law enforcement to publicize *Net Cetera*, and

By 2009, 75 percent of teens had cell phones, giving them additional ways to conduct online activities such as e-mailing and accessing social networking sites. © Lezlie Sterling/Sacramento Bee/Getty Images.

the agency has distributed more than 3.7 million copies of the guide since it was introduced in October 2009. The FTC will continue to work with other federal agencies, state departments of education, school districts, and individual schools to distribute *Net Cetera* and OnGuardOnline.gov to parents and educators. Additionally, the FTC plans to reach out to other groups that work with kids, such as summer camps, state education technology associations, and scouting organizations to publicize these materials.

In furtherance of the FTC's education efforts, commission staff also participated in the Online Safety and Technology Working Group (OSTWG), a working group composed of private sector members and federal agencies. OSTWG reported its findings about youth safety on the Internet to Congress on June 4, 2010. Among its tasks, OSTWG reviewed and evaluated the status of industry efforts to promote online safety through educational efforts, parental control technology, blocking and filtering software, and age-appropriate labels for content. With respect to

Internet safety education, OSTWG recommended greater inter-agency cooperation, publicity, and public-private sector coop-eration for projects such as OnGuardOnline and *Net Cetera* to improve their national uptake in schools and local communities. As described above, the FTC is actively working to expand the reach of the already successful OnGuardOnline and *Net Cetera* projects. . . .

Social Networking

Social networking is pervasive among teens: 73 percent of American teens ages 12 to 17 now use social networking sites such as Facebook and MySpace, up from 55 percent two years ago. Nearly half of teens use these sites on a daily basis to interact with their friends. Teens use social networking to send messages to friends, post comments, and share photos and videos.

The commission has sought to protect teenage and other con-sumers in this environment through law enforcement, research, and education. It has brought a number of enforcement actions against social networking sites since 2006, when social network-ing exploded on the youth scene. Most recently, the commission announced a consent order against Twitter, Inc., settling charges that it falsely represented to consumers that it would maintain reasonable security of its system and that it would take reason-able steps to ensure that private tweets remain private. Under the order, Twitter has agreed to maintain reasonable security and to obtain independent audits of its security procedures every two years for 10 years. The commission also has brought actions against several social networking sites that targeted youth but failed to adhere to the Children's Online Privacy Protection Act (COPPA) with respect to users under the age of 13. The commis-sion will continue to examine the practices of social networking sites and bring enforcement actions when appropriate.

In addition to its enforcement work, the commission has been gathering information about social networking as part of a recently concluded series of public roundtables on consumer

MOST TEENS TEXT FRIENDS DAILY

Percentage of teens who contact their friends daily by different methods, by age.

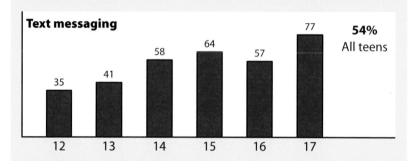

Text messaging

54% All teens

12	13	14	15	16	17
35	41	58	64	57	77

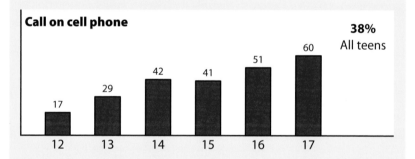

Call on cell phone

38% All teens

12	13	14	15	16	17
17	29	42	41	51	60

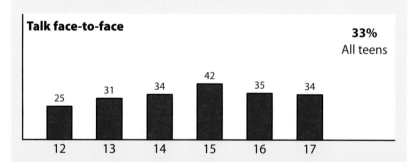

Talk face-to-face

33% All teens

12	13	14	15	16	17
25	31	34	42	35	34

'All teens' refers to all teens ages 12–17.

MOST TEENS TEXT FRIENDS DAILY (continued)

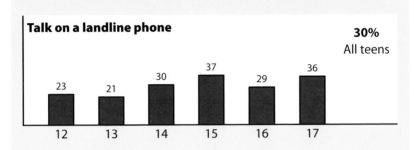

Talk on a landline phone

30%
All teens

23 — 12
21 — 13
30 — 14
37 — 15
29 — 16
36 — 17

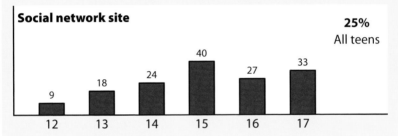

Social network site

25%
All teens

9 — 12
18 — 13
24 — 14
40 — 15
27 — 16
33 — 17

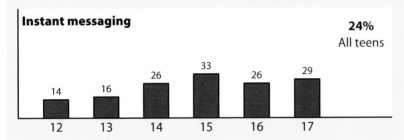

Instant messaging

24%
All teens

14 — 12
16 — 13
26 — 14
33 — 15
26 — 16
29 — 17

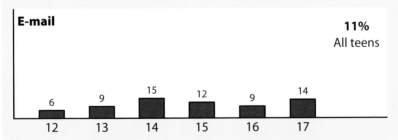

E-mail

11%
All teens

6 — 12
9 — 13
15 — 14
12 — 15
9 — 16
14 — 17

Taken from: Amanda Lenhart, "Teens, Cell Phones and Texting: Text Messaging Becomes Centerpiece Communication," Pew Internet and American Life Project, April 20, 2010. pewresearch.org.

privacy. The goal of the roundtables was to explore how best to protect consumer privacy without curtailing technological innovation and beneficial uses of information. Participants at the roundtables repeatedly raised issues related to social networking, and a specific panel was devoted to the subject. Experts on this panel discussed the difficulty of defining consumer expectations on social networking sites, issues related to third-party applications that use data from social networking sites, and the effectiveness of privacy disclosures and privacy settings in the social networking space. . . .

Mobile Technology

Teens' use of mobile devices is increasing rapidly—in 2004, 45 percent of teens ages 12 to 17 had a cell phone; by 2009, that figure jumped to 75 percent. Many teens are using their phones not just for calling or texting, but increasingly for applications like emailing and web browsing, including accessing social networking sites and making online purchases. They are also using relatively new mobile applications that raise unique privacy concerns, such as location-based tracking.

The FTC has been actively addressing privacy issues relating to mobile technology for several years. In 2008, the commission held a town hall meeting to explore the evolving mobile marketplace and its implications for consumer protection policy. Participants in the meeting examined topics such as consumers' ability to control mobile applications and mobile commerce practices targeting children and teens. In April 2009, FTC staff issued a report setting out key findings and recommendations based on the town hall meeting. Having highlighted that the increasing use of smartphones presents unique privacy challenges regarding children, the town hall meeting led to an expedited regulatory review of the Children's Online Privacy Protection Rule. The review is taking place this year [2010], even though it was originally set for 2015.

More recently, the privacy roundtable discussions devoted

a panel to addressing the privacy implications of mobile computing. This panel focused on two significant issues: the extent to which location-based services were proliferating in an environment without any basic rules or standards, and the degree to which transparency of information-sharing practices is possible on mobile devices. As with social networking, the commission staff's upcoming report [issued in preliminary form in December 2010] on the privacy roundtables will further address these issues.

In addition to these policy initiatives, the FTC is ensuring that it has the tools necessary to respond to the growth of mobile commerce and conduct mobile-related investigations. In the past month [June 2010], the FTC has expanded its Internet lab to include smartphone devices on various platforms and carriers. The commission also has obtained the equipment necessary to collect and preserve evidence from these mobile devices. With these smartphones, FTC staff can now improve its monitoring of unfair and deceptive practices in the mobile marketplace, conduct research and investigations into a wide range of issues, and stay abreast of the issues affecting teens and all consumers. . . .

Privacy Models and Teens

The issues surrounding teens' use of digital technology raise the question whether there should be special privacy protections for them. Some have suggested that COPPA's protections be extended to cover adolescents between the ages of 13 and 18; others suggest that separate privacy protections should be established for teens.

The COPPA statute and implementing regulations enforced by the FTC require operators to provide notice to, and receive consent from, parents of children under age 13 prior to the collection, use, or disclosure of such children's personal information on websites or online services. In the course of drafting COPPA, Congress looked closely at whether adolescents should be covered by the law, ultimately deciding to define a "child" as an individual under age 13. This decision was based in part on the view that most young children do not possess the level of knowledge or judgment to make appropriate determinations about when and if to divulge personal information over the Internet. The FTC supported this assessment.

While this parental notice and consent model works fairly well for young children, the commission is concerned that it may be less effective or appropriate for adolescents. COPPA relies on children providing operators with parental contact information at the outset to initiate the consent process. The COPPA model would be difficult to implement for teens, as they have greater access to the Internet outside of the home than young children do, such as in libraries, friends' houses, or mobile devices. Teens seeking to bypass the parental notification and consent requirements may also be less likely than young children to provide accurate information about their age or their parents' contact information. In addition, courts have recognized that as children age, they have an increased constitutional right to access information and express themselves publicly. Moreover, given that teens are more likely than young children to spend a greater proportion of their time online on websites that also appeal to adults, the practical difficulties in expanding COPPA's reach to adolescents might unintentionally burden the right of adults to engage in online speech.

The commission will continue to evaluate how best to protect teens in the digital environment and take appropriate steps to do so. In specific instances, there may be opportunities for law enforcement or advocacy in this area. For example, just this week [in July 2010], the commission's Bureau of Consumer Protection sent a letter to individual stakeholders in XY corporation, which operated a now-defunct magazine and website directed to gay male youth. The letter expressed concern about these individuals' efforts to obtain and use old subscriber lists and other highly sensitive information—including names, street addresses, personal photos, and bank account information from gay teens. The letter warns that selling, transferring, or using this information would be inconsistent with the privacy promises made to the subscribers, and may violate the FTC Act; thus, the letter urges that the data be destroyed.

More generally, the FTC believes that its upcoming privacy recommendations based on its roundtable discussions will greatly benefit teens. The commission expects that the privacy proposals emerging from this initiative will provide teens both a greater understanding of how their data is used and a greater ability to control such data. Finally, the commission is available to work with this committee, if it determines to enact legislation mandating special protections for teens.

The commission is committed to protecting all consumers in the digital environment, especially those consumers, such as teens, who are particularly vulnerable to threats on the Internet. The FTC will continue to act aggressively to protect teens through education, law enforcement, and policy initiatives that will better enable teens to control their information online.

> "It is possible to protect kids [online] while protecting speech."

Young People and Free Speech Can Be Protected on Social Networks

Stephen Balkam

Stephen Balkam is the founding chief executive officer of the Family Online Safety Institute in Washington D.C. In the following viewpoint, Balkam argues that lawmakers must be cautious in enacting cyberbullying legislation. He insists that criminalization may not eradicate the problem and may infringe free speech. Most instances of teasing and making mean comments, he contends, differ from actual harassment and are part of normal adolescent behavior, which negatively affects some teens and not others. Instead of strict regulation, government officials, educators, and parents should teach students digital citizenship skills and social media literacy, the author concludes.

If Wikipedia is to be believed, cyberbullying involves "the use of information and communication technologies to support de-

Stephen Balkam, "Protecting Kids While Protecting Free Speech," First Amendment Center, March 31, 2009. Copyright © 2009 by First Amendment Center. All rights reserved. Reproduced by permission.

liberate, repeated and hostile behavior by an individual or group that is intended to harm others." Cyberbullying has eclipsed sexual predators on the Internet as the number one concern of policymakers, parents and kids themselves. It is a growing phenomenon taking many forms and is perpetrated on a growing range of platforms, devices, sites and Web-based services.

With the advent of this new technology, schoolyard behavior such as teasing and starting rumors can continue to affect a child's day long after the school day is over. Text and instant messaging, Twittering and MySpace postings are the new playground for adolescents. The increasing use of technology to bully creates a dilemma for parents, legislators and educators trying to deal with the cyber-savvy schoolyard bully who, rather than picking a physical fight, now uses MySpace.

One third of teens using the Internet have experienced online harassment. This is a growing concern for families dealing with the emotional impact of bullied children, and it is also a problem for legislators trying to take action to stop the harmful effects of this behavior.

Cyberbullying, not surprisingly, has the greatest impact on teens spending a large portion of their time online and teens creating Internet content about themselves. A Pew Internet and American Life study found that teens "who share their identities and thoughts online are more likely to be targets than are those who lead less active online lives."

The Centers for Disease Control and Prevention studied cyberbullying and found, "It's difficult to say how severe online harassment is as a public health issue, because a posting or e-mail that might upset some children is shrugged off by others." This is not to say that cyberbullying does not cause problems. While some students report no impact from online harassment, cyberbullying can have a negative effect on others. "Consistent with previous research, youth who are harassed online report a mix of psychological problems. They are significantly more likely to be targeted by victimization offline." Some students may be upset because of what is said to them online, and these feelings may carry over into their performances at school or interactions with classmates.

Legislators and educators need to be aware that teasing or making mean comments is different than actual harassment. Authorities shouldn't react to middle school drama with intense regulation but should be proactive and try to prevent the conflicts. Criminalizing cyberbullying won't solve the problem.

News Headlines Make Bad Laws

In the past few years, several high-profile cases emerged and created a loud cry for legislation to punish cyberbullying rather than address the actual problem. Vermont, for example, recently enacted anti-cyberbullying legislation after Ryan Halligan, a 13-year-old Vermont student, was taunted online and at school and committed suicide in 2003.

The most high-profile case is that of Megan Meier, a troubled Missouri teen who took her life after being harassed online by [a classmate's mother, who pretended to be] a teenage boy. This case may be more unique than what most teens face because the person behind the bullying was an adult. What is also different is that Lori Drew, the perpetrator of the computer hoax, was not charged with a crime related to her bullying behavior; instead, she was charged under a "federal statute designed to combat computer crimes that was used to prosecute what were essentially abuses of a user agreement on a social networking site." The prosecutor in the Meier case may have been overreaching by using this computer hacking law to punish bullying [a judge ultimately overturned a jury's guilty verdict on misdemeanor charges in this case].

There are additional high-profile examples of cyberbullying contributing to the psychological problems of teens, but a handful of tragedies should not be used to quickly push through laws that may punish but not eradicate the problem of cyberbullying.

Representative Linda Sanchez introduced legislation that would have provided stiff penalties for cyberbullying, but it failed to pass into law. © Chip Somodevilla/Getty Images.

Respond Quickly—Legislate Slowly

Lawmakers should proceed cautiously before enacting legislation governing off-campus speech that does not "substantially interfere" with school activities. School districts have the most authority to intervene with cyberbullying when the actions occur on school property or on the school computer network. Currently, some states have adopted laws that criminalize cyberbullying or use school discipline codes to punish students for online behavior occurring off campus and after school time.

States with higher-profile cases tend to have more stringent anti-cyberbullying legislation passed in reaction to the publicity of a cyberbullying case. If there is going to be legislation at all, there should be a national definition of the problem and a uniform way to address it. States must be aware that there is potential danger of infringing on free-speech rights of students through current and proposed legislation.

There could also be jurisdiction problems from criminalizing cyberbullying in some states, but not in others. In the Megan

Meier case, Missouri prosecutors determined that Lori Drew had not violated any local laws, but federal prosecutors used the location of the MySpace servers to charge Drew in California. If bullying occurs via social-networking sites in states without cyberbullying statutes, students might face disciplinary action or criminal charges based on the server location.

U.S. Rep. Linda Sanchez [a Democrat from California] introduced legislation in 2008 to criminalize cyberbullying. The Megan Meier Cyber-bullying Prevention Act called for a fine or imprisonment of up two years for cyberbullying (H.R. 6123, 110th [Congress 2nd Session, 2008]). This legislation, which was referred to a House subcommittee but failed to pass, ensured that only "severe, repeated, and hostile behavior" should be punished. The bill, however, went too far by making imprisonment a punishment for cyberbullying.

Do we really want to criminalize what is, sadly, fairly normal adolescent behavior? Lawmakers need to be cautious not to criminalize posting embarrassing pictures or spreading rumors, and must not restrict speech any more than necessary Legislation should focus on alternatives to punishment and encourage educational solutions.

Technology as a Problem and a Solution

Text messaging, social networking and online video sharing extend the boundaries of the schoolyard. As students adapt to changing technology, cyberbullying will continue to be a problem. Advances in technology allow students to bully others after school, but the technology also improves students' knowledge. Students need to learn better digital citizenship and how to use technology not as a weapon but as a resource.

The Internet industry is working to do more than just monitor Web sites and take down offensive material. Industry leaders are involved in groups to evaluate the problems and work with researchers and others to discuss solutions. There are software programs available for parents to keep track of what their kids are doing online, and most social-networking and video-sharing Web sites have policies against harassment and ways to report abuse [according to Jennifer Lawinski in a 2008 article on foxnews.com]: "Tech companies are releasing new software products that monitor and police kids' Internet use, helping them avoid cyber-bullying and letting parents know when it's occurring." Wider use of such programs could provide a technical rather than legislative solution to thwart cyberbullying.

Legal or technological fixes alone, however, won't eliminate cyberbullying. There needs to be increased industry efforts, in-

Dealing with Cyberbullies May Be Easier than Dealing with Bullies Offline

The good news is that dealing with online harassment or bullying can be easier for teens than facing an offline bully. Teens can literally ignore people on instant messenger by making themselves "invisible," blocking specific e-mails, creating a new e-mail account or profile, or reporting incidents to their ISP [Internet Service Provider]. Lots of teens who responded to [a] Tagged.com survey said they either blocked or ignored teens or adults who were bothering them online. In many cases, just doing this is enough to shut down online tormentors. It's also fairly easy for ISPs to track down where e-mail is coming from if the bully is attempting to do it anonymously. And because the bully is putting everything in writing in e-mail, text messages, or instant messages, teens or parents can save and print their "digital paper trail," providing a full account of what happened to school administrators, the bully's parents, or the police.

Anastasia Goodstein, Totally Wired: What Teens and Tweens Are Really Doing Online, New York: St. Martin's Griffin, 2007.

creased education for students and increased resources for parents to ensure their families are practicing Web safety.

Alternatives to State Regulation— Creating a Culture of Responsibility

There are many non-government alternatives to regulation. Parents, educators, government officials and students can work toward a culture of responsibility where everyone takes on differing, but overlapping, areas of responsibility. It is more useful to educate students to make wise choices online than to regulate every aspect of their lives. Such an approach would protect free speech. In addition, teaching digital citizenship skills can have a positive impact on youth, and media-literacy training can help kids learn how to block harmful messages, protect personal information and report abuse.

Parents play a key role in this culture of responsibility because they need to learn how children use technology and need to be aware of problematic behavior. The CDC [Centers for Disease Control and Prevention] suggests, "For years parents and caregivers have been asking their children where they go and who they are going with when they leave the house. They should ask these same questions when their child goes online."

If there are serious problems with cyberbullying, there are also serious civil consequences available. If harassment occurs to such a degree that a student's reputation is ruined or he suffers severe emotional consequences, the bullied student could bring a defamation action or sue for intentional infliction of emotional distress.

President Barack Obama's administration should call for funding to be used for cyberbullying prevention, and the president should call an online-safety summit to learn more about cyberbullying and promote a national education campaign to eliminate it.

It is possible to protect kids while protecting speech. With the right legislation aimed at education and technological solutions, the harmful impact of cyberbullying can be reduced. Together, educators, legislators, the . . . administration, parents and students can create a culture of responsibility where free speech is preserved but cyberbullying is minimized.

> "Because the Supreme Court has not yet
> addressed this particular issue, courts
> are struggling to define the proper place
> of so-called student Internet speech."

Court Rulings on Social Networks, Teens, and Free Speech Rights Are Unclear

Michael J. Kasdan

In the following viewpoint, Michael J. Kasdan contends that recent court rulings regarding student speech on social networks are contradictory. Drawing from Supreme Court cases that defined the authority of schools to regulate disruptive speech on campus and at school activities, the Court of Appeals for the Third Circuit handed down conflicting decisions for students who created false, demeaning online profiles of principals, Kasdan states. In his opinion, this authority should not be extended to cover Internet speech off campus, as it curtails the First Amendment and the potential of disruption is vague. Kasdan is an associate at the law firm Amster, Rothstein & Ebenstein in New York.

The move toward online communication has the potential to throw off the historically careful balance that has been struck

Michael J. Kasdan, "Student Speech in Online Social Networking Sites: Where to Draw the Line," *IP and Entertainment Law Ledger*, November 22, 2010. Copyright © 2010 by Michael J. Kasdan. All rights reserved. Reproduced by permission.

regarding First Amendment issues in the realm of "student speech." In a seminal trilogy of cases, the Supreme Court balanced the free speech rights of students with school districts' ability—and even responsibility—to regulate student speech that disrupts the learning environment. Before the proliferation of instant messaging, SMS texts [phone, web, or mobile texting], and social networking sites, the Court allowed schools to regulate on-campus speech in limited circumstances (i.e., when the speech disrupts the learning environment) but did not extend the school's authority to regulate speech that occurs off campus (i.e., speech subject to traditional First Amendment protection). Electronic communication blurs the boundary between on- and off-campus speech. While a student may post a Facebook message from the seeming privacy of his or her own home, that message is widely accessible and could have a potentially disruptive effect on campus.

Because the Supreme Court has not yet addressed this particular issue, courts are struggling to define the proper place of so-called student internet speech. Indeed, two different Third Circuit panels recently came to exactly opposite conclusions on the very same day about the ability of schools to regulate student internet speech: in one, the Third Circuit upheld a school's ability to discipline a student for creating a fake MySpace profile mocking the school's principal; in the other, the Third Circuit held the school could not regulate conduct (again, creation of a fake MySpace profile about the school's principal) that occurred within the student's home. Both opinions have since been vacated pending a consolidated rehearing *en banc* [a session in which the entire membership of the court will participate in a decision], but the message is clear: courts throughout the country require guidance on the appropriate legal principles applicable to student internet speech.

The remainder of this [viewpoint] introduces the relevant Supreme Court precedent, explores in greater depth the two contradictory Third Circuit opinions, and offers some preliminary analysis as to how the Third Circuit (and perhaps ultimately the Supreme Court) may clarify the law in the pending *en banc* decision.

Background—Supreme Court Precedent

The Supreme Court's seminal pronouncement that set the limits of a school's ability to regulate student speech came down in 1969. In *Tinker v. Des Moines Independent Community School District,* the Supreme Court addressed the issue of "First Amendment rights, applied in light of the special characteristics of the school environment." The Court reasoned that while students do not

"When my kids get out of line, I threaten to start a 'My Space' page and invite their friends."

"When my kids get out of line, I threaten to start a 'My Space' page and invite their friends," by Marty Bucella. www.CartoonStock.com.

"shed their constitutional rights to freedom of speech or expression at the schoolhouse gate," the right to free speech must be balanced against the interest in allowing "[s]tates and . . . school officials, consistent with fundamental constitutional safeguards, to prescribe and control conduct in the schools." The so-called *Tinker* rule holds that in order for a school district to suppress student speech (by issuing a punishment or discipline relating to that speech), the speech must materially disrupt the school, involve substantial disorder, or invade the rights of others: "conduct by the student, in class or out of it, which for any reason— whether it stems from time, place, or type of behavior—materially disrupts class work or involves substantial disorder or invasion of the rights of others is, of course, not immunized by the constitutional guarantee of freedom of speech."

Since *Tinker*, the Supreme Court has addressed free speech issues in the context of schools in several cases. In each case, the Court addressed the tension between the students' right to free expression and the schools' need to regulate school conduct in favor of the schools. In *Bethel School District v. Fraser*, the Court distinguished *Tinker* and found that a school's discipline of a student for his sexual-innuendo-charged assembly speech was not a violation of the student's First Amendment rights. More recently, in *Morse v. Frederick* [June 25, 2007], the Court held that the First Amendment does not prevent school officials from suppressing student speech that was reasonably viewed as promoting illegal drug use at a school-supervised event.

Today's Online Student Speech Cases

The degree to which student online speech may be regulated is an increasingly significant issue. As stated in a recent *New York Times* article, "the Internet is where children are growing up. The average young person spends seven and a half hours a day with a computer, television, or smart phone . . . suggesting that almost every extracurricular hour is devoted to online life." And today's online speech has some distinguishing characteristics from "ordinary speech." It is extremely public. It may be rapidly distributed to a wide group of people extremely quickly. And it may potentially be saved forever.

A recent series of cases demonstrate that courts are grappling with how to apply the Supreme Court free speech precedent to student speech that has moved to online mediums such as the now-ubiquitous Facebook or Twitter. None of the triumvirate of Supreme Court student speech cases maps easily to the arena of online student speech. As one state supreme court noted,

> Unfortunately, the United States Supreme Court has not revisited this area [of the First Amendment rights of public school students] for fifteen years. Thus, the breadth and contour of these cases and their application to differing circumstances continues to evolve. Moreover, the advent of the Internet has complicated analysis of restrictions on speech. Indeed, *Tinker's* simple armband, worn silently and brought into a Des Moines, Iowa, classroom, has been replaced by [today's students'] complex multi-media websites, accessible to fellow students, teachers, and the world.

A recent series of cases from the Third Circuit demonstrates the complexities raised by these cases. In one case, a Third Circuit panel found a school's discipline of a student for his online speech to be a violation of the First Amendment and that the school's authority could not extend to such off-campus behavior. That very same day, a different Third Circuit panel addressing an almost identical fact pattern came to the opposite conclusion, finding no First Amendment violation when a school district punished a student for online speech.

Recent Online Student Speech Cases

J.S. ex rel. Snyder v. Blue Mountain School District In *J.S.* [sometimes referred to as *Snyder*], the Third Circuit affirmed a district court ruling that a school district had acted within its authority in disciplining a student for creating an online profile on her MySpace page that alluded to "sexually inappropriate behavior and illegal conduct" by her principal.

The student was a 14-year-old eighth-grader who, along with a friend, had been disciplined by the principal for a dress code violation. A month later, the students [used a home computer to create a fictitious profile on MySpace for the principal]. The MySpace profile, which included a picture of the principal taken from the school's website, described him as a pedophile and a sex addict whose interests included "being a tight ass," "[having sex] in my office," and "hitting on students and their parents." Word of the MySpace profile soon spread around school. Eventually, the principal found out about it. In response, the principal issued the students a ten-day suspension for violating the school's rule against making false accusations against members of the school staff.

The students' parents sued the school district, claiming that the suspension was a violation of their children's First Amendment rights. The district court disagreed and found for the school board, concluding that the school had acted properly in suspending the students and that their First Amendment rights had not been violated.

On appeal, the Third Circuit affirmed. The panel majority noted that although the Supreme Court "has not yet spoken on the relatively new area of student internet speech," courts can derive the relevant legal principles from traditional student speech cases, such as *Tinker, Bethel,* and *Morse.* Drawing from the *Tinker* standard that a school may discipline students for speech that "create[s] a significant threat of substantial disruption" within the school, the Third Circuit found that discipline was appropriate and permissible based primarily on the fact that the profile targeted the principal in a manner that could have undermined his authority by referencing "activities clearly inappropriate for a Middle School principal and illegal for any adult." The court also found that the online context of the speech, which allowed for quick and widespread distribution, exacerbated the situation and increased the likelihood of "substantial disruption."

A pair of court cases came to opposite conclusions on the same day about whether schools have the authority to punish students for making inflammatory parody profiles on MySpace. © AP Images/News Sentinel, Jeff Adkins.

In a strongly written dissent, one of the panel judges concluded that the *Tinker* standard had not been met: *Tinker* requires a showing of "specific and significant fear of disruption, not just some remote apprehension of disturbance." While acknowledging the general power of school officials to regulate conduct at schools, the dissent concluded that the majority decision vests school officials with dangerously over-broad censorship authority in that it "adopt[s] a rule that allows school officials to punish any speech by a student that takes place anywhere, at any time, as long as it is about the school or a school official . . . and is deemed 'offensive' by the prevailing authority." The dissent further noted that "[n]either the Supreme Court nor this Court has ever allowed schools to punish students for off-campus speech that is not school-sponsored and that caused no substantial disruption at school."

Layshock v. Hermitage School District Curiously, a different panel of judges of the Third Circuit reached the opposite conclusion on the very same day in a similar case, *Layshock v. Hermitage School District*. In *Layshock*, the Third Circuit panel affirmed a district court ruling that Hermitage School District's suspension of high school student Justin Layshock for his "parody profile" of the high school principal on his MySpace page was improper. The *Layshock* panel concluded that the high school's discipline of the student for his online behavior violated his First Amendment free speech rights and that the school's authority did not reach such off-campus behavior.

The student, a 17-year-old high school senior, created a fake MySpace profile in the name of his principal, using a picture of the principal from the school's website. The profile mocked the principal, indicating that he was a "big steroid freak," a "big hard ass" and a "big whore" who smoked a "big blunt." When the principal learned of the profile, he issued a ten-day suspension and barred Justin from extracurricular activities for disruption of school activities, harassment of a school administrator over the Internet, and computer policy violations.

Layshock's parents sued the school district and the principal, asserting violations of the First and Fourteenth Amendments. The district court ruled in their favor on the First Amendment claim, concluding that the school was unable to establish "a sufficient nexus between Justin's speech and a substantial disruption of the school environment, which is necessary to suppress students' speech per *Tinker*."

On appeal, the Third Circuit agreed that "it would be an unseemly and dangerous precedent to allow the state in the guise of school authorities to reach into a child's home and control his/her actions there to the same extent that they can control that child when he/she participates in school sponsored activities." The court refused to allow the school district to exercise authority over a student "while he is sitting in his grandmother's home after school."

On April 9, 2010, shortly after issuing the seemingly contradictory rulings in *J.S.* and *Layshock*, the Third Circuit agreed to rehear the two cases *en banc*. Given the factually similar circumstances of the two cases and their opposite results, it is not surprising that the Third Circuit found it necessary to provide clear guidance delineating what type of speech may be punished and how far school districts may go in punishing online speech. Argument was heard by the full court on June 3, 2010, and a ruling is expected sometime this year. [The court ruled on behalf of the students in June 2011.] The Third Circuit *en banc* review of the *J.S.* and *Layshock* cases may also be a precursor to a Supreme Court pronouncement on the topic of school regulation of online student speech.

Clarifying the Law?

One key issue raised in these *en banc* appeals—and in other cases around the country addressing similar issues—is whether online speech by a student that is generated off school property and not during school hours, but is nonetheless directed at the school, can be regulated by a school district at all. That is, is such speech "student speech" that may be regulated under appropriate circumstances or is it "off-campus speech" that is out of the reach of school regulation under *Tinker, Bethel,* and *Morse?*

In the *en banc* appeals, the school districts argued in their briefing papers and at oral argument that the Supreme Court's reasoning in *Bethel* regarding the ability of schools to regulate disruptive student speech should likewise apply to online speech that is directed at school faculty. They argued that although such "speech" may be created outside of school, it is student speech, because it is specifically aimed at the school or a school administrator. Further, they argued that such speech may be restricted because it has a sufficient impact on the proper functioning of the school. The districts reason[ed] that because students today create, send, and access communication using multiple methods including online social media sites, email, and text messaging, the proper focus is not where the speech was made, but whether its impact is felt in school.

On the other hand, the students argued that a school district's ability to regulate disruptive student speech should not extend to speech outside of school and that the curtailment of students' off-campus speech is doctrinally indefensible.

In my view, extending school districts' intentionally limited authority to off-campus speech—whether online or otherwise— would set a dangerous precedent. Indeed, during oral argument of the *en banc* appeals in June, Chief Judge McKee of the Third Circuit asked if a group of students could be punished if they were overheard in a baseball stadium calling their principal a "douchebag." The clear answer is no. Judge Rendell similarly noted that "the First Amendment allows people to say things that aren't nice." These seem to be the right points to be making. In other words, how are the online profiles in the *J.S.* and *Layshock* cases any different than distasteful jokes or mocking speech about school officials made outside of school? The *Tinker-Bethel-Morse* trilogy of cases allows for limited regulation of speech in school; they simply do not contemplate otherwise limiting speech outside of school. While online speech undoubtedly has some characteristics that distinguish it from Judge McKee's example—i.e., a mocking online profile can be rapidly accessed by a wide group of students and lasts longer than the spoken word—these differences do not justify redrawing the line in order to allow a school to regulate a student's out-of-school online speech.

A second key issue is, if schools were allowed to regulate such speech, how substantial must a disruption be to be considered a "substantial disruption" for which discipline is permitted? Is a school district's judgment that there is potential to cause disruption enough, or should more be required?

The school districts argue that they should have the authority to regulate speech when it is reasonably foreseeable that it would cause a substantial disruption in school. But the students argue that if a school district is authorized to punish students' off-campus online speech based on a presumed "reasonable possibility" of future disruption, this would eviscerate the careful balance drawn in *Tinker*.

In my view, if schools are allowed to regulate online off-campus speech merely because it is directed towards school officials (a dubious proposition under Supreme Court First Amendment precedents), it is critical that this authority remain as limited as possible. One way to do that is to tie the school's authority to the presence of an in-school disruption. Giving schools the authority to determine that, in their view, there is a "reasonable potential" for a future disruption, even if there is no evidence of any disruption, seems to give them too much power. For instance, in the Third Circuit cases discussed above, it seems likely that anyone who viewed the fake MySpace profile would know it was intended as a joke. And there was no evidence of any disruption at all. Still, the school district punished the speech. This gives the school district too much power to discipline speech that occurs off-campus.

The principles set forth in the seminal Supreme Court student speech cases should favor the students in online speech cases—unless the courts adopt the view that online speech is inherently different from traditional speech. If so, then the rules regarding school regulation of student speech will change in turn. The Third Circuit *en banc* cases—and perhaps one day the Supreme Court—must now grapple with that issue.

| *"You can't punish someone for the conduct and words of another person."*

Teens with Websites May Not Be Liable for Content by Third Parties

Thomas A. Jacobs

Thomas A. Jacobs was a judge pro tem and commissioner in the juvenile and family courts for the Maricopa County Superior Court in Arizona and is the author of several books on youth rights, including Teen Cyberbullying Investigated: Where Do Your Rights End and Consequences Begin? *In the following viewpoint excerpted from* Teen Cyberbullying Investigated, *Jacobs discusses a court case wherein a student, Ryan Dwyer, was not held liable for negative comments others posted about a school administrator on Dwyer's site. The author states that the district court ruled that visitors to Dwyer's site, which provided a warning against threats, were content creators liable for their actions. Therefore, Jacobs advises teens with their own sites to post similar disclaimers, but to also review or edit comments before publishing.*

Thomas A. Jacobs, J.D., Excerpted from *Teen Cyberbullying Investigated: Where Do Your Rights End and Consequences Begin?* Copyright © 2009. Used with permission of Free Spirit Publishing Inc., Minneapolis, MN: 800-735-7323; www.freespirit.com. All rights reserved.

Welcome to the Anti-Maple Place— Your Friendly Environment

This was Ryan Dwyer's greeting on the Web page he created at home. Ryan was 14 and in 8th grade at Maple Place School in New Jersey. His site included an About page, Favorite Links, and a Guestbook. His About page contained his own comments about school, such as:

- It's fun to disrupt class, especially in Mrs. Hirshfield's room!
- Start protests, they aren't illegal.
- MAPLE PLACE IS THE WORST SCHOOL ON THE PLANET!
- Wear political T-shirts to annoy the teachers.
- Use your First Amendment right wisely.
- THIS PAGE PROTECTED BY THE U.S. CONSTITUTION.

Ryan's Favorite Links contained links to music groups, body piercing sites, and sites devoted to the constitutional rights of public school students. His Guestbook invited visitors to post their own messages and comments. Ryan warned guests against profanity and threats:

"Please sign my guestbook but NO PROFANITY AT ALL!!!!!!! and no threats to any teacher or person EVER. If you think it may be a bad word or it may be threatening DO NOT TYPE IT IN."

Ryan later stated that he created the site because he felt he had no voice at school. "You need your First Amendment rights to get change," he later stated at a news conference.

Due to the applications he used, Ryan had no control over messages posted on his site. He wasn't able to edit any posts and could only delete the entire Guestbook. Several visitors used profanity and ethnic slurs, and others made threats against the school and the principal. "The principal is a fat piece of crap," one declared. "He should walk his fat ass into oncoming traffic."

The principal saw the site and called the police. Ryan was suspended for five days and removed from the baseball team for one month. He was also excluded from a class trip to Philadelphia. He and his parents challenged the discipline imposed and asked the district court to intervene. . . .

What the Court Decided

In 1996, Congress passed the Communications Decency Act, which applies to this case. In part, it states that anyone who creates a Web site is not responsible for information added to it by other sources. In other words, you can't punish someone for the conduct and words of another person. This means that the visitors to Ryan's Guestbook became content providers and were held accountable for their own comments. Under the law, Ryan was not responsible for their postings.

If Ryan's own comments on his Web site constituted a true threat, they were unprotected speech. The school could punish him without violating his free speech rights. The court stated that "in light of the violence prevalent in schools today, school officials are justified in taking very seriously student threats against faculty or other students." In Ryan's case, however, there was no evidence that the material that Ryan posted on his site was intended to threaten anyone or manifest any violent tendencies. The comments made by others in his Guestbook are not attributable to Ryan.

Did Ryan's Web site disrupt the school? If it did, he could be disciplined. But the disruption had to be more than the discomfort or unpleasantness that accompanies an unpopular [point of view], as previous cases ruled. The mere fact that content causes hurt feelings or resentment does not render the expression unprotected. The court found no disruption caused by Ryan's online expression.

Although ruling in Ryan's favor, the court did not decide the issue of money damages against the principal and school superintendent. Those issues were left for a jury to decide. However,

Comment Control

Most blog-publishing tools have several administrative options for managing comments. Choosing the right setup for a Comments section can be a personal preference but can also be determined by the goals of the blog.

Allowing or disabling comments is an option you might have on your blog-publishing tool. Ask yourself the following questions to get a sense of whether your blog should contain comments.

What reason for blogging best reflects your goals?
　　a. To put my thoughts and ideas out there and see what happens.
　　b. To build a following or community.
　　c. To create a personal publishing project.

> *Aliza Sherman Risdahl,* The Everything Blogging Book: Publish Your Ideas, Get Feedback, and Create Your Own Worldwide Network, *Avon, MA: Adam Media, 2006.*

an agreement was reached and the school district agreed to pay Ryan $117,500 for damages and attorney fees.

Following the settlement, Ryan said, "While my parents and I are happy the case is resolved, most importantly, I'm hopeful this will help ensure that free speech rights of students aren't trampled on again."

How Does This Decision Affect You?

This case covers an issue not addressed by other cases. When you create a Web page, you have the option of inviting others to comment on it. You can limit this to approved friends, or you can open it up to the world. Either way, you have no control over what others will say. Ryan tried to keep it clean by including a direct warning.

Ryan Dwyer, left, was suspended for derogatory comments made by a visitor to his website's guestbook. A high court held that Dwyer could not be held responsible for someone else's words. © AP Images/Brian Branch-Price.

The bottom line: Depending on the applications you are using, you may not be able to control what others post on your Web page. It's advisable to add a warning to posters and monitor your page closely. Keep in mind, however, that even if you include a warning, people may post material on your site that could possibly lead to school disruption or other charges.

What Is Ryan Doing Now? Ryan graduated from high school and attends William and Mary College in Virginia.

Related Cases

Larson v. Birdville High School (Texas, 2005) Kelsey Larson was a freshman cheerleader at Birdville High School in Texas. In 2005, one of her friends posted a derogatory statement about other cheerleaders on Kelsey's Xanga blog. School officials claimed it violated the code of conduct for cheerleaders, and Kelsey was kicked off the team. She and her parents fought the discipline and won. Kelsey returned to the team the next semester.

Goldsmith and Morgan v. Brookwood High School (Georgia, 2003) Lloyd Goldsmith Jr. and Edward Morgan were senior honor students at Brookwood High School in Georgia. In 2003, they commented about one of their teachers on another student's Web site. Lloyd described a fictional assault on the teacher and wrote, "Filthy whore's gotta die!" Edward added that he wanted to impale the teacher with a fence post. He later retracted the comment saying it was meant as a joke. Both students were suspended and ordered to complete community service hours. The boys and their parents sued the school district [and asked] that all disciplinary action be removed from their records. The case was settled out-of-court with the district agreeing to clear the students' records and pay each $95,000.

Curzon-Brown v. Lathouwer (California, 2000) Ryan Lathouwer had a frustrating semester at San Francisco City College. Tired of the unpredictable quality of teachers and classes, he started a private Web site called "Teacher Renew." The site allowed students to post evaluations of their teachers using an A through F scale. Users could also post comments anonymously. Ryan did not edit posted reviews, giving students free reign of the site. In less than a year, the site had nearly 18,000 hits. Ryan commented, "Most of the reviews are positive—the derogatory ones are students' opinions and they have a right to voice their opinions, even if it's not in the most intelligent way." When brought to his attention, Ryan removed offensive material from the site.

English professor Daniel Curzon-Brown was angered by reviews that rated him as one of the 10 worst teachers at the college. His ratings also included profane language and attacked his sexual orientation. He sued Ryan and the college for defamation and sought an order preventing future defamatory reviews. Just before trial, the professor agreed to dismiss his lawsuit and pay part of Ryan's legal fees. It became apparent to him that he did not have a winning case. The settlement was considered a major victory for free speech on the Internet, and for student media everywhere.

Things to Think About

If you have your own Web site, profile page, or blog, do you have control over the comments or postings others add to it? Does your page include a disclaimer or warning about profanity or offensive comments? If you can edit comments before posting them, how do you decide what's ethical or decent? If you question whether someone's comment is appropriate, is it sometimes better to leave it out all together? These are some questions to ask yourself as you sign on to social networking sites and participate in online discussions.

> *"Facebook's administrators have the right to take down any user profile that they discover is fake."*

Defamation and Fraudulent Profiles on Social Networks

Chris Gatewood

In the following viewpoint, Chris Gatewood describes how a fake profile on a social network may or may not be found defamatory, or contain a false statement that damages a person or group, by the courts. Gatewood explains that the First Amendment protects a satirical or parodying profile too bizarre or extreme to be believed, unless it is perceived to be created by the subject. Nonetheless, social networks may remove such profiles, under their terms of use, in order to avoid litigation, he says. Gatewood is an intellectual-property lawyer at the firm Hirschler Fleischer in Richmond, Virginia.

You've built a social networking web site, and your online community is going from strength to strength. Great! But hang on a minute—you've received a request to remove content that one of your users has posted. Where do you stand? And who is legally responsible for that content?

Chris Gatewood, "Fake User Profiles: Free Speech or Defamation?," SitePoint, November 7, 2008. Copyright © 2008 by SitePoint. All rights reserved. Reproduced by permission.

The Right to Free Speech

Most SitePoint readers are probably aware that, in the United States at least, the law protects the free speech of online publishers and users when it comes to the critique or parody of a person or business. But where is the line drawn for slander or defamation? And if you own or manage a social networking site, what course of action should you follow when someone demands that you take down a fake profile?

Several US courts have explored this very question recently: lawsuits have been brought by an assistant principal in Texas, a high school dean in Indiana, and the president of a small town in Illinois (apparently towns in Illinois have presidents). Each case has made its way through the court system, and the judges or juries concerned have had to consider First Amendment free speech arguments—as well as the content of the fake profiles—to decide if the spoofers have crossed the legal line and are defaming their targets.

Impostor Profiles Are Likely Here to Stay

Under current law, impostor profiles and other objectionable Web content are here to stay, at least until social networking Web sites take the responsibility of setting up effective verification procedures.

But it's not likely that will happen, said one attorney knowledgeable in the topic, because Web sites potentially open themselves to a greater risk of prosecution by trying to verify all postings than by verifying none.

David Wood, "No Easy Remedy for Imposter Postings on Social Networking Sites," ConsumerAffairs.com, March 17, 2008.

But first thing's first—what exactly *is* defamation?

Defamation is a false statement of fact that creates a damaging, negative image of a person or a group. (Libel is the written form of defamation, while slander refers to a spoken slur.) Statements of opinion are not defamation, and statements that are unlikely to be believed are also unlikely to support a legal claim. Beyond those basics, however, the law varies somewhat from country to country. In the United States, the plaintiff must prove that an allegedly defamatory statement is false. However, in England, the statement is assumed to be false unless it's proven by the defendant to be true. The contrast in where the burden of proof lies with these two countries is just one example of how the interests of free speech and personal reputation are balanced in different ways throughout the world.

The First Amendment to the US Constitution, and the court cases decided under it, define the extent of free speech rights in the US. Public figures, in particular, should expect to endure a great deal of criticism before a court will restrict an individual's right to make statements about them. And although the potential impact of the statements are magnified by the reach of the Internet, the legal analysis of what is in bounds and what is clearly out-of-bounds is substantially the same as if it were printed on fliers under windshield wipers.

Hustling for the Right to Satirize

One famous court case in the United States in 1988, *Hustler Magazine v. Falwell,* tested the limits for how far a satirical statement can go before it constitutes defamation. The case involved television evangelist Jerry Falwell and *Hustler* magazine, owned by pornographer Larry Flynt.

The *Hustler Magazine v. Falwell* case explored exactly where the line between freedom of speech and defamation exists: once a statement is deemed to have crossed that line, it loses its free speech protection. *Hustler* ran a fake ad in the magazine making fun of a series of ads where famous people talked about their "first time" trying a certain brand of liquor. Those ads were double-edged, and suggested that the people were also talking about their other "first time." Flynt and his crew decided to place Reverend Falwell in their satirical version of the ad, and concocted some fairly cheeky suggestions about the nature of the reverend's "first time." It was harsh, but as far as Flynt was concerned, that was the point. Not amused, Falwell sued for defamation.

Falwell argued that the fake ad was so outrageous that it should not be protected as permissible free speech. However, the US Supreme Court ruled that, because public figures like Falwell are subject to all sorts of commentary—even provocative satire—and because the trial court had decided that the statements were too extreme to be believable, the statements were not defamatory. Instead, the parody was deemed protected speech that Flynt and his crew had the right to make, just as if it had been a political cartoon.

Is that Really You, Mister President?

One important aspect of a defamation case is whether a false statement about someone *is likely to be believed*. If the statement is perceived to be too strange to be credible, then the court will rule that readers will understand it to be a joke. Even if it's a rude joke, if it's deemed probable that the readers will interpret it as a joke, then the publisher is unlikely to be successfully sued for defamation.

However, if the false content appears to have been posted by the target of the parody, then the site's readership is more likely to believe the false statements. For example, a fake online profile on a social networking site—where the person appears to be making statements about themselves—could fall into this category.

One recent example involved the assistant principal and students of a high school in San Antonio, Texas. The students posted a fake profile of the assistant principal on MySpace, which contained false information about her sexual orientation and practices, as well as obscene comments and content.

Dr. Jerry Falwell sued Hustler *magazine over a parody ad that cast the religious leader in a negative light. The Supreme Court ruled that the ad was protected speech because it was so exaggerated that no one was likely to believe it.* © Jeff Fusco/Getty Images.

If readers viewed the page believing it was posted by the assistant principal herself, then there is an issue of harm to the teacher's reputation, hence why the defamation law exists in the first place. MySpace took the page down when they were notified that the assistant principal herself had not posted the profile. The aggrieved administrator decided to pursue the students who were involved, resulting in disciplinary action by the school. She also filed a lawsuit against two of the students and their parents, with allegations of defamation, libel, and negligent supervision. Interestingly, the lawsuit does not include MySpace as a defendant; the publisher's prompt action of removing the profile—in this case—kept them from being tied up in the lawsuit.

Researching the precise line between free speech protection and defamation is probably not within the legal budget of most web developers. So what should you do if such an issue comes up on your social networking site? My advice is to consider following the lead of MySpace in the Texas case—keep it simple and stay out of the way.

In response to a recent spate of complaints about fake user profiles, Facebook representatives issued a statement reminding members of their terms of use, where to "impersonate any person or entity" was strictly prohibited.

This means that Facebook's administrators have the right to take down any user profile that they discover is fake. All web sites and applications that implement a degree of social networking would do well to follow Facebook's example. By including a similar clause [among] your own terms and conditions, you could prevent a possible defamation action arising from user content.

> "The digital revolution has altered what the very act of copying means; however, a more than 30-year-old analog copyright law remains in effect."

Copyright Laws Must Be Changed for Youths and Students on the Internet

J. Patrick McGrail and Ewa McGrail

In the following viewpoint, J. Patrick McGrail and Ewa McGrail argue that copyright laws have not kept pace with the Internet, all but prohibiting the use of protected digital material for instructional purposes and casual sharing and remixing by youths. Fair use exemptions, the authors contend, allow for limited use, but do not provide guidelines for the Web or distance learning. Consequently, they recommend that the laws are revised to let youths legally transform or borrow parts of songs, images, and videos in creative ways and support online education. J. Patrick McGrail is an assistant professor of communication at Jacksonville State University in Florida. Ewa McGrail is an associate professor of language and literacy at Georgia State University.

J. Patrick McGrail and Ewa McGrail, "What's Wrong with Copyright: Educator Strategies for Dealing with Analog Copyright Law in a Digital World," *Innovate*, vol. 5, no. 3, 2009. Copyright © 2009 by Nova Southeastern University. All rights reserved. Reproduced by permission.

Article I, Section 8, Clause 8 of the U.S. Constitution states that "to promote the Progress of Science and useful Arts, by securing for limited Times to Authors and Inventors the exclusive Right to their respective Writings and Discoveries," Congress may pass laws to protect the intellectual property of the citizens of the United States. Today, the controlling statute of copyright, Title 17, Chapter 1, Section 102, covers books, graphical material, written music, manuscripts, paintings, architecture (in the form of plans), and sculpture as well as various forms of musical, dramatic, pictorial, and motion picture work and sound recordings. This title of U.S. Code comprises all of U.S. copyright law, including the Copyright Act of 1976 (effective January 1, 1978).

The 1976 Act, now more than 30 years old, is the current law of the land with regard to copyright. The act gives remarkably broad protection to authors, requiring only that a creative work be fixed in a "tangible means of expression," such as a tape, disc, hard drive, or piece of paper. This means that copyright protection is sweeping, potentially covering artifacts as quotidian as e-mails, laundry lists, and love notes. Online, such activities as downloading a Web page for later reference or posting a video made while the television plays in the background, may constitute violations of copyright. Since the act was passed, the digital age has fundamentally reshaped the relationship between original works and their copies that held with the analog duplication processes of the former era. This transformation has created a host of legal, ethical, and social circumstances that the 1976 law could not anticipate.

In this [viewpoint], we explore how the technological, social, cultural, and legal developments of the digital age challenge educators and students who seek to make use of copyrighted material for educational purposes and offer educators strategies for dealing with today's copyright challenges. We conclude with a call to revise the copyright law and suggest the direction that a revised copyright law should take to support responsible, creative use of both traditional and new media content, both within and beyond the physical walls of the classroom.

Copyright and Today's Students

Digital transmission transforms the act of copying in two ways. First, digital technology enables mass copying; e-mail and Internet technologies allow users to send high-quality copies of graphical, visual, or musical materials to a huge number of recipients. Second, generation loss disappears; that is, each copy is precisely the same as any other copy. Indeed, if the work in question begins in the digital realm (as is the case with today's digital audio recorders, camcorders, and cameras), not only does every copy exactly resemble every other copy, but each copy is also precisely similar to the original. In this context, the essential difference between the original and a copy—the *raison d'être* [the reason for its existence] for copyright law—becomes nothing more than a legal fiction.

Educators struggle with these changes on the front lines as they are confronted with the task of educating young people about the boundaries of a copyright law that, when read conservatively, prohibits virtually all of the casual copying and remixing in which students often engage. According to [researchers A.] Lenhart and [M.] Madden, today's content creators are mostly young people who generate material for a wider Internet audience, branching outside of traditional educational venues to disseminate their content on personal Web sites, blogs, and various other kinds of sites, such as chat rooms and social networking sites. In doing this, they borrow from the work of many other creators, choosing many different kinds of content to mix, such as cartoons, manga and anime, background tracks, and movie clips, including those originally produced and those found.

Although industry groups such as the Record Industry Association of America (RIAA) and the Motion Picture Association of America (MPAA) run advertisements that attempt to equate unauthorized duplication with the theft of physical objects, such as cars and clothing, the targets of these ads, young people, have been slow to amend their behavior. [Researchers P.] Aufderheide, [P.] Jaszi, and [N.B.] Brown found that undergraduate and graduate college students who crewed online video content were "universally under-informed and misinformed about [copyright] law." However, a study by University College London's CIBER [Centre for Information Behaviour and the Evaluation of Research] group on information behavior by adults and children (ages 12–15) concluded that rather than indicating a lack of knowledge about the basic principles of intellectual property, the evidence revealed that young people demonstrated "a collapse of respect for copyright."

Some of this collapse may be attributed to the inadequacy of current copyright law with respect to the Web 2.0 applications that young people have increasingly embraced. These applications, which take their power from user-created and user-shared content, encourage young people to share both content they have created themselves, whether from scratch or by remixing, and content they have found or borrowed. Young people's heavy involvement in these Web-based sharing technologies has fostered an eagerness to share data, photographs, music, and movies with little concern for the legal status of these items.

The Growing Power of Copyright

The Copyright Act of 1976 has been augmented by the passage of three amendments to the original law, the first two of which give original content creators even broader rights. The first is the Sonny Bono Copyright Term Extension Act of 1998, which extends the protected life of certain popular works that were about to fall into the public domain, including that most famous of fictional characters, Mickey Mouse. The second is the Digital Millennium Copyright Act (DMCA) of 1998, which imposes stern new penalties both for unauthorized copying and for circumventing technologies designed to protect content. The third is the Technology Education and Copyright Harmonization (TEACH) Act of 2002,

What Content Is in the Public Domain?

- works published before January 1, 1923.
- works published between 1923 and 1978 that did not contain a valid copyright notice.
- works published between 1923 and 1978 for which the copyright was not renewed.
- works authored by employees of the federal government.
- works that the copyright owner has freely granted to the public domain.

Linda Starr, "Copyrights and Copying Wrongs,"
Education World, *May 25, 2010.*
www.educationworld.com
/a_curr/curr280a.shtml.

the only bright spot for educators in these amendments, which grants certain permissions to nonprofit educational institutions for the limited transmission of digital course materials beyond those allowed by the fair use doctrine.

Considered separately, none of these amendments seems unreasonable. However, taken together, several aspects of the amended law create the potential for disturbing scenarios for educators. First, these amendments make violation of copyright not merely a civil tort settled by the concerned parties in a civil proceeding, but potentially a federal criminal offense under the jurisdiction of the Federal Bureau of Investigation. The DMCA, in particular, grants rights holders extraordinary powers of administrative subpoena that permit them to force institutions that are the alleged conduit of the infringement, such as universities, to produce personal information about perceived perpetrators—often, students.

The second disturbing element of current copyright law is that nothing in it prevents a powerful rights holder, such as the RIAA, from pursuing an infringement case against a perceived violator even if that "violator" reasonably believes—or even has been advised by legal counsel—that he or she is acting under the aegis of fair use as defined by copyright law. This is because fair use is a set of guidelines only; it leaves room for a range of interpretations as to what is and is not permissible. As a result, universities have endeavored to protect themselves by requiring faculty members and students to adhere to sometimes rigid policies that often do not reflect the actual content of the law.

Of course, not every alleged violator is worthy of the attention of a wealthy or influential rights organization. Trade groups such as the MPAA or the RIAA are interested in protecting the content of their member organizations; they strategically pursue court action in order to send a message to perceived violators. Because the law specifies that infringement may be vicarious or contributory, a university may be legally construed by the copyright owner as engaging in contributory infringement if it fails to take reasonable measures to curtail the flow of copyrighted material onto the hard drives of its students and employees. Copyright holders sometimes mount "deep pocket" attacks directed at an institution (for example, a university) that has significant financial resources in order to score both a financial and a public relations victory. In cases against individuals, the rights organization typically demands a sum of money, sometimes in the thousands of dollars, to settle the matter out of court. Many impecunious students have taken the deal and settled, as was the case in the 2007 litigation brought against 40 Indiana University students. Once again, the rationale is to score a public relations victory and get the word out that violations will not be tolerated.

The Limitations of Fair Use

At the same time, fair use exemptions from copyright, intended to allow limited use of copyrighted materials for the purposes of education, journalism, commentary, criticism, scholarship, and research, have not adapted well to the digital era. In fact, as [former teacher and editor Linda] Starr maintains, there are no fair use guidelines for using the latest digital technologies to support the needs of content creators, some of whom are students, and of consumers, who are also often students; the old guidelines restrict both the audience and the publication venue for multimedia educational projects created with copyrighted material to a closed classroom space and a course or school audience. Fair use standards also do not recognize the for-profit online classroom as a legitimate venue. The most expansive definition of fair use covers only uses "by instructors or pupils in the course of face-to-face teaching activities of a nonprofit educational institution, in a classroom or similar place devoted to instruction" (Title 17, Chapter 1, Section 110, U.S. Code). Although the TEACH Act . . . makes clear that fair use allows for limited uses of copyrighted audiovisual materials in virtual classrooms, these virtual spaces do not enjoy the same level of protection afforded to the face-to-face classroom.

Additionally, while educators are able to use many types of audiovisual material under fair use in face-to-face educational settings and, in a somewhat more restricted way, in distance learning, students are considerably more constrained in their ability to use material to comment on the media world around them, especially when they seek to do so for audiences and venues outside the classroom. Today's technologies enable students to produce material on the Internet for an audience that potentially includes anyone with Internet access. The irreverent, critical, highly commentative content that students produce and publish on weblogs, videoblogs, podcasts, and YouTube makes liberal use of satire. Creators in these venues borrow from and ape the icons of contemporary visual culture, often by utilizing snippets of the material that is the target of their commentary. All of this use is potentially in violation of current copyright law in spite of the fact that, as [author and academic] Stephen Marshall shows, creating new work from previously existing material creates value.

Changing the Copyright Law

Changes in copyright law are unquestionably needed to address these challenges to education. The question is exactly what those changes should look like. We make the following tentative recommendations while also urging that educators themselves engage thoughtfully in copyright reform efforts. With 83% of higher education institutions now providing distance learning opportunities in at least some of their programs, distance learning is likely to flourish alongside traditional physical universities. With this in mind, we believe that the disconnect between what is permitted in face-to-face teaching and what is allowed in distance education needs to be remedied. It is neither fair nor practicable to expect educators to treat the presentation of course content and the work of students differently based on whether the student is physically present or is attending class via a virtual learning environment.

Changes should also be made to address the ways in which contemporary copyright law constrains the creative options open to students. We suggest the reconsideration of regulations on transformative content. Borrowing a line, a snippet of a song, or a picture and transforming it in order to comment on the underlying material, we contend, does not interfere in any significant way with the commercial potential of the original. If anything, if proper attribution is given to the original sources, it may make people more aware of the original. With this as well as the educational value of creating such commentary in mind, broader rules for commentative, parodic, and satiric matter must be considered.

What Educators Can Do

The first step an educator should take is to become aware of recent developments in copyright reform. Consumer organizations,

Mitch Bainwol, former chairman and CEO of the Recording Industry Association of America (RIAA), stands before the organization's logo. The Digital Millennium Copyright Act gives powerful rights holders such as the RIAA broad latitude to pursue lawsuits against those who violate copyright laws, even inadvertently. © Stephen J. Boitano/Getty Images.

librarians, researchers, and educators have begun to realize how easy it is to run afoul of copyright law in everyday professional activities, and the unlikelihood of being caught is cold comfort. A little proactive behavior on the part of educators—for example, contacting relevant copyright reform organizations or e-mailing legislators—can go a long way toward shaping meaningful change. Educators should also be aware that they have colleagues in library science, research, and even politics who strenuously maintain that current copyright law is, at the very least, impermissibly vague. Organizations and conferences, such as the Electronic Frontier Foundation, the Association of Research Libraries, and the Conference on Fair Use (CONFU), have produced significant, concrete suggestions for amending the law, each taking a somewhat different view of what needs to be fixed.

In the meantime, educators must be realistic and assume

that current copyright law will remain the controlling structure for some years into the future. Students who may want to use previously existing work must be provided with alternatives. Educators should encourage students to create projects entirely from original work, which may be both creatively liberating and legally prudent. Students might also work from preexisting pieces that are copyright free. Several new audio software programs, such as Garage Band and Soundtrack, provide small snippets of copyright-free musical material that may be blended and mixed in different ways to create original work, which may then be copyrighted by the student user. Other programs like Ableton Live and Fruity Loops (recently renamed FL Studio) offer similar functionality for more professional users. On the visual side, camcorders have become inexpensive and many cell phones have video capability; applications like Apple's iMovie make digital film editing easy. In this environment, there are few barriers to students creating their own motion pictures from the ground up.

As students engage in creating their own original work, they would benefit from some discussion of the intellectual property issues involved in online and face-to-face communication and information sharing (for educational purposes and otherwise) and common misconceptions regarding copyright law. Georgia Harper's crash course in copyright might be a useful resource for facilitating such a conversation. Creative Commons offers an alternative view of copyright, presenting a variety of available licenses that preserve copyright while allowing the creator to define what kinds of reuse is allowable. Such conversations will engender more respect for intellectual property and encourage more responsible uses of it in online creations, broadening the vision of what copyright can be and prompting students to recognize that they too can be creators with copyrights that are valid and enforceable. A third and rather more difficult issue that educators must unite to address is the changing nature of the classroom and its ramifications for copyright law. Today's educators may reasonably want to make limited use of copyright-protected materials in the creation of wikis, blogs, videoblogs, or Second Life avatars for educational purposes. This would rarely result in substantial commercial harm to a copyright holder's interests, yet according to current copyright regulations, these virtual venues for learning must not include copyright-protected material.

As this [viewpoint] goes to press, a bill is languishing in the U.S. House of Representatives, HR 1201, the Freedom and Innovation Revitalizing U.S. Entrepreneurship Act of 2007 (the FAIR USE Act), sponsored by Congressman Rick Boucher [a Democrat from Virginia]. This bill, which has the support of numerous copyright reform organizations, will codify some of the Copyright Office's suggestions regarding fair use so that, as a matter of law, clearly defined fair use exemptions will not be subject to litigation by copyright holders.

The copyright challenges discussed in this [viewpoint] have resulted from the law's failure to keep pace with technology and technology's impact on society. In subtle ways, the digital revolution has altered what the very act of copying means; however, a more than 30-year-old analog copyright law remains in effect. This situation presents vexing legal difficulties for a variety of stakeholders, educators being one of the most important. We urge educators to consider our recommendations and to be proactive in the movement for better copyright law, including supporting the passage of HR 1201 and remaining engaged in the legislative process. At the same time, educators must work to help students understand both the strictures and the opportunities of copyright.

Organizations to Contact

The editors have compiled the following list of organizations concerned with the issues debated in this book. The descriptions are derived from materials provided by the organizations.

American Library Association (ALA)
50 E. Huron Street, Chicago, IL 60611
(800) 545-2433
website: www.ala.org

ALA is the oldest and largest library association in the world, with more than 65,000 members. Its mission is to promote the highest quality library and information services and public access to information. ALA offers professional services and publications to members and nonmembers. The association supports the use of social networking sites in libraries and classrooms as a part of economic, cultural, civic, and cultural life.

Center for Democracy and Technology (CDT)
1634 I Street NW, #1100, Washington, DC 20006
(202) 637-9800 • fax (202) 637-0968
website: www.cdt.org

CDT's mission is to develop public policy solutions that advance constitutional civil liberties and democratic values in new computer and communications media. Pursuing its mission through policy research, public education, and coalition building, the center works to increase citizens' privacy and the public's control over the use of personal information held by government and other institutions. Its publications include issue briefs, policy papers, and CDT Policy Posts.

Center for Safe and Responsible Internet Use (CSRIU)

474 W 29th Avenue, Eugene, OR 97405
e-mail: contact@csriu.org
website: www.cyberbully.org

CSRIU provides research and outreach services to address issues of the safe and responsible use of the Internet. It provides guidance to parents, educators, librarians, policy makers, and others regarding effective strategies to assist young people in gaining the knowledge, skills, motivation, and self-control to use the Internet and other information technologies in a safe and responsible manner.

Cyberbullying Research Center

Sameer Hinduja, School of Criminology and Criminal Justice, Florida Atlantic University
5353 Parkside Drive, Jupiter, FL 33458-2906
e-mail: hinduja@cyberbullying.us
website: www.cyberbullying.us

Launched in 2002 by professors Sameer Hinduja and Justin W. Patchin, the center's website serves as a clearinghouse of information concerning the ways adolescents use and misuse technology. It is intended to be a resource for parents, educators, law enforcement officers, counselors, and others who work with youth, and to offer facts, figures, and detailed stories from individuals who have been directly affected by online aggression. In addition, the site includes numerous resources to help prevent and respond to cyberbullying incidents.

Electronic Frontier Foundation (EFF)

454 Shotwell Street, San Francisco, CA 94110-1914
(415) 436-9333 • fax: (415) 436-9993
e-mail: information@eff.org
website: www.eff.org

EFF is an organization of students and other individuals that aims to promote a better understanding of telecommunications issues. It fosters awareness of civil liberties issues arising from advancements in computer-based communications media and supports litigation to preserve, protect, and extend First Amendment rights in computing and telecommunications technologies. EFF's publications include the electronic newsletter *EFFector Online* and online bulletins and publications, including *First Amendment in Cyberspace.*

Federal Trade Commission (FTC)

600 Pennsylvania Avenue, NW, Washington, DC 20580
(877) 382-4357 (FTC-HELP)
website: www.ftc.gov

The FTC deals with issues that touch the economic life of every American. It is the only federal agency with both consumer protection and competition jurisdiction in broad sectors of the economy. Its website offers information on online privacy and security issues such as identity theft, Internet fraud, and protecting kids online and on social networks. It maintains OnGuard Online.gov.

Internet Society (ISOC)

1775 Wiehle Avenue, Suite 102, Reston, VA 20190-5108
(703) 326-2120 • fax: (703) 326-9881
e-mail isoc@isoc.org
website: www.isoc.org

A group of technologists, developers, educators, researchers, government representatives, and businesspeople, ISOC supports the development and dissemination of standards for the Internet. It also works to ensure global cooperation and coordination for the Internet and related Internet-working technologies and applications. It publishes the *IETF Journal*, a newsletter, and annual reports.

National Crime Prevention Council (NCPC)

2001 Jefferson Davis Highway, Suite 901, Arlington, VA
22202
(202) 466-6272
website: www.ncpc.org

NCPC's mission is to be the nation's leader in helping people keep themselves, their families, and their communities safe from crime. To achieve this end, NCPC produces tools that communities can use to learn crime prevention strategies, engage community members, and coordinate with local agencies. Its website includes information on cyberbullying.

National School Safety Center (NSSC)

141 Duesenberg Drive, Suite 7B, Westlake Village, CA
91362
(805) 373-9977
e-mail: info@schoolsafety.us
website: www.schoolsafety.us

NSSC serves as an advocate for safe, secure, and peaceful schools worldwide and as a catalyst for the prevention of school crime and violence. It provides school communities and their school safety partners with quality information, resources, consultation, and training services. The center offers books, videos, and resource papers.

National Youth Rights Association (NYRA)

1101 15th St. NW, Suite 200, Washington, DC, 20005
(202) 835-1739
website: www.youthrights.org

NYRA is a youth-led national nonprofit organization dedicated to fighting for the civil rights and liberties of young people. NYRA has more than 7,000 members representing all 50 states. It seeks to lower the voting age, lower the drinking age, repeal curfew laws, and protect student rights.

For Further Reading

Books

Anupam Chander, Lauren Gelman, and Margaret Jane Radin, eds., *Securing Privacy in the Internet Age.* Stanford, CA: Stanford Law Books, 2008.

Jessie Daniels, *Cyber Racism: White Supremacy Online and the New Attack on Civil Rights.* Lanham, MD: Rowman & Littlefield, 2009.

Sameer Hinduja and Justin W. Patchin, *Bullying Beyond the Schoolyard: Preventing and Responding to Cyberbullying.* Thousand Oaks, CA: Corwin Press, 2009.

David Kirkpatrick, *The Facebook Effect: The Inside Story of the Company That Is Connecting the World.* New York: Simon & Schuster, 2010.

Lawrence Lessig, *Remix: Making Art and Commerce Thrive in the Hybrid Economy.* New York: Penguin Press, 2008.

Viktor Mayer-Schonberger, *Delete: The Virtue of Forgetting in the Digital Age.* Princeton, NJ: Princeton University Press, 2009.

Gustavo Mesch and Ian Talmud, *Wired Youth: The Social World of Adolescence in the Information Age.* New York: Routledge, 2010.

Zizi Papacharissi, *A Networked Self: Identity, Community, and Culture on Social Network Sites.* New York: Routledge, 2010.

Daniel J. Solove, *The Future of Reputation: Gossip, Rumor, and Privacy on the Internet.* Ann Arbor, MI: Caravan Books, 2007.

Nancy E. Willard, *Cyberbullying and Cyberthreats: Responding to the Challenge of Online Social Aggression, Threats, and Distress.* Champaign, IL: Research Press, 2007.

Periodicals and Internet Sources

Lisa Barone, "How Not to Get Sued for Stealing Content on the Internet," *Business Insider*, February 4, 2011.

Barbie Clark, "Friends Forever: How Young Adolescents Use Social-Networking Sites," *Intelligent Systems*, November/December 2009.

Brendan Collins, "Privacy and Security Issues in Social Networking," *Fast Company*, October 3, 2008.

The Economist, "Privacy 2.0: Give a Little, Take a Little," January 28, 2010.

Greg Ferenstein, "Why Banning Social Media Often Backfires," Mashable.com, April 13, 2010.

Geoffrey H. Fletcher, "Power Up, Don't Power Down: Barring Students from Using Cell Phones, MySpace, and Other Communication Technologies Once They Enter the Classroom Is the Wrong Approach," *Technical Horizons in Education*, September 1, 2006.

Eric Goldman, "The Law of Social Networking Sites: A Primer," FindLaw, May 15, 2007.

Scott D. Marrs and John W. Lynd, "Viral Videos Publicize—But Infringe," *National Law Journal*, May 8, 2006.

Kurt Opsahl, "A Bill of Privacy Rights for Social Network Users," www.eff.org, May 19, 2010.

Helen A.S. Popkin, "Hey, Kids! Hate School? Don't Tell Facebook," msnbc.com, October 6, 2009.

Sunsara Taylor, "The Culture that Killed Tyler Clementi," *Revolution Online*, October 7, 2010.

Perry Viscounty, Jennifer Archie, Farnaz Alemi, and Jenny Allen, "Social Networking and the Law," *Business Law Today*, March/April 2009.

Amanda L. Williams and Michael J. Merten, "A Review of Online Social Networking Profiles by Adolescents: Implications for Future Research and Intervention," *Adolescence*, Summer 2008.

David Wood, "No Easy Remedy for Imposter Postings on Social Networking Sites," ConsumerAffairs.com, March 17, 2008.

Index

"Websense" (filter), 32
Wei, Molly, 6
West Valley Christian School
(West Hills, CA), 36
Wikipedia, 100
Willard, Nancy, 65
Cyberbullying and Cyberthreats:
Responding to the Challenge
of Online Social Aggression,
Threats and Distress, 49
World Wide Web, 4
Wu, George H., 5

X

Xanga, 22, 123
XY Corporation, 98

Y

Yahoo, 30
YouTube, 14
Young Adult Library Services
Association, 31

Z

Zellis, David W., 21